# Your Inner Butterfly

## Karen Sorbo

# Your Inner Butterfly

## Embracing, Releasing and Re-writing Your Story

## Karen Sorbo

SWIFT·LAUNCH
PUBLISHING

ISBN: 979-8-218-69487-6

COMPANIES, ORGANIZATIONS, INSTITUTIONS, AND INDUSTRY PUBLICATIONS: Quantity discounts are available on bulk purchases of this book for reselling, educational purposes, subscription incentives, gifts, sponsorship, or fundraising. Special books or book excerpts can also be created to fit specific needs such as private labeling with your logo on the cover and a message from a VIP printed inside.

**For more information on the Karen Sorbo Foundation, visit www.karensorbofoundation.com**

Photo by Kelsey Lee Photography

Swift Launch Publishing
18110 Dorman Rd.
Lithia, FL 33547

# Table of Contents

## Dedication

As a self-proclaimed "Daring" woman, I must admit that writing this book was one of the scariest endeavors I have ever set out to accomplish. As you will gather within the pages of this book, I grew up without any encouragement, acknowledgment, or recognition for anything I ever felt led to be and do. However, I have learned through the years that one need not seek approval or recognition to be worthy. The value that we all seek is already within you when you follow your heart and your passion. No one but you and God need to reaffirm that you are enough, that you are special, and that you really matter in this life.

While attempting to write my first book, I learned more about who I am than ever before. I learned that the ones who hurt you the most can make a bigger impact on the development of your character than those that praise you. You must be the one who decides you will develop a strong and beautiful character that resonates love for all.

In complete gratitude, I dedicate this book to my late father, Kermit Anderson. Even though he never believed in me and criticized me his entire life, making me feel like I did not matter, I am so grateful for him. Why? This allowed me to use my pain and reach out to help others hurting even more than me. Once you reach inside yourself, grab ahold of that pain, and turn it around, it enables you to grow in wisdom, understanding, and love. Love those that hurt you, understand that they are hurting too, and through your forgiveness, perhaps they may come to know the truth. In doing this, you will feed your own soul and grow to realize you need no one and nothing else to make you feel perfect the way God created you. You matter in this world.

I love you, Dad for what I have been able to learn from you. I now love those who have hurt me, and in return for that love, I have grown into a woman of great character who finds deep compassion in everything I do.

Compassion: first, last, and always.

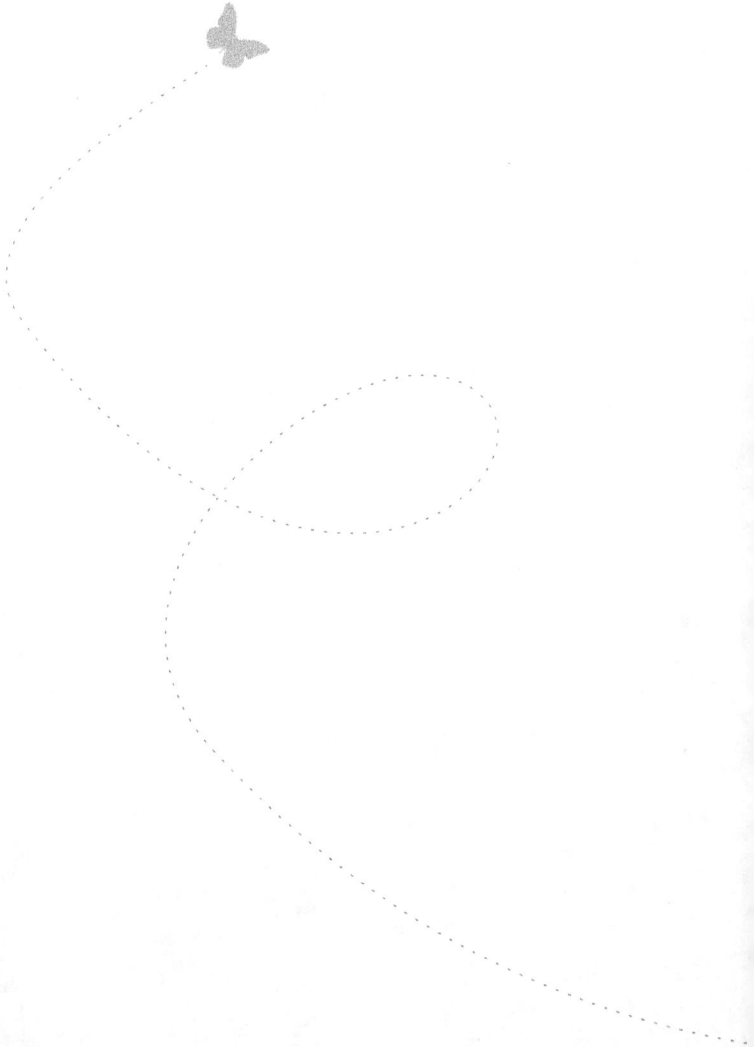

## Introduction

If you take a true story, add raw emotion, embrace the experience, and allow space for reflection, you will gain wisdom.

**Story – Emotion – Experience – Reflection – Wisdom**

It is for this reason that I wrote this book, with the hope of adding value to your life through the stories and lessons contained hereafter. We all have a story, the golden thread that is the culmination of all our experiences, some worse than others. I certainly know that there are many out there who have gone through far worse than I. When we embrace the idea that our past stories had a purpose specially designed for each of us, then we can begin to re-write the way we viewed and perceived that which has happened to us, into that which has happened for us.

It is my hope that as I tell the healing pain and joy in my life story, you will see the same in yours. As I express the valleys and peaks of my emotions, you will find peace in your own. As I describe trials and challenges of my experiences, you will draw knowledge and inspiration from them. And, as I pause to slowly reflect, you will relate with others and do the same; through this, perhaps much deeper relationships will be built.

**Tell – Express – Describe – Pause – Relate**

I hope this book will serve you and will be used as a conversation piece with your closest friends.

Adding wings to Caterpillars

does not create Butterflies; it

creates awkward and dysfunctional

caterpillars. Butterflies are created

through transformation.

— Stephanie Marshall

# 1

## Love Sparks

**MY STORY** begins in a small town, rural Minnesota hobby farm. Everywhere you looked there were cages or pens with some kind of animal, and we were surrounded by life! It was a unique environment that allowed God to plant the seeds in my heart that would eventually make me the woman I am today.

We had a simple life, far from extravagant, but we rarely went without. On any given day, you could come and see turkeys strutting, chickens pecking, ducks quacking, rabbits hopping, and many other critters that kept us all busily entertained.

For most of my childhood, my father was in charge of raising us kids. I was the youngest of three, and even though I was the only girl, I was treated like a third boy. My father was a manly man to say the least, so I was never "Daddy's little girl." I was more like the third and last boy on the farm. The further we get into this story, the more you will see how my relationship with my father created a foundational piece of my life experience that formed the woman I am today.

Fortunately and unfortunately, the demands my father placed on us prevented my siblings and me from experiencing a normal childhood. I have been told that before the age of 6, I never really spoke much at all. I was seldom allowed to express my feelings, so the only thing I felt I could do was be a quiet observer.

## *National Geographic* Inspiration

At the young age of 8, I experienced a turning point in my life. I don't mean anything dramatic like the clouds parting or an angel appearing to me, but for the first time in my life, I felt God was revealing his plan for me, and I embraced it.

I remember going to the dentist that year. While in the waiting room, I discovered my first *National Geographic* magazine. This simple magazine represents the genesis of God's inspiration and strength pouring from Him to me. God used that magazine to spark a flame inside of me that has yet to burn out. In fact, it has only grown bigger ever since.

For the first time in my life, I saw vivid pictures and examples of how the less fortunate in the world live. Page after page of my *National Geographic*, I looked at images of starving children all over the world, living in huts with no electricity or running water. Their bellies were distended from malnutrition and worms. Some pictures were dreadful to look at, but in retrospect, there was something emerging from me as I read this magazine; my world-view was broadened.

Through this magazine, my heart was captured and permanently lit on fire. I simultaneously had my spirit provoked and my soul touched. As I reflect on this turning point in my life, it reminds me that God is always chasing us. His primary goal is to win our hearts and restore our relationship with Him in order to better serve the world through a labor of love. One of the ways He captures our hearts is by revealing our true hidden desires that reside in the unchecked places of our spirit.

I encourage you to examine the ways and the tools with which God has captured your heart. This is no small matter. In fact, matters of the heart are the only things that matter. I am sharing with you the story of how God captured my heart, but what is the love story of your life? Where have you experienced little love sparks that you may have brushed off? What fills your heart with zeal, stirs your mind, and provokes you to action? There is something there. Just keep asking and keep reading...The more I read in my new magazine, the more I wanted to share it with others and find ways to simply help. So, I did the unthinkable. I grabbed the magazine after my dental appointment was over, and I stuffed it down my shirt. I could not wait to get home and thumb through more pages of this glorious world I had just discovered. There was much more to life than on the farm. My father eventually found me with this magazine. He actually never asked me where I got it but was insistent on scolding me with the words, "Karen, you will never have the opportunity to go to these places, and even if you did, what do you think you are going to do, save the world?"

The response I received from my parents isn't much different from the response the world may give you when you try to change it. Many parents try to shelter their kids from heartbreak by not letting them dream. Sure, the kids won't get heartbroken, but they also won't learn to love either. Despite my parents' efforts to shelter my heart the best way they knew how, I begged them to buy me a subscription to this magazine. They eventually gave in. It was one of the first big sales of my life.

## Philanthropic Barbie

Little girls idolize Barbie dolls because that is what they want to become – beautiful, admired, and wanted. Even though I had those longings as well, my heart was telling me I wanted to be more than just a pretty doll. I wanted to be the *National Geographic* Barbie who helped little children by giving them food, hope, love, and an opportunity.

This opened the floodgates of my desire, and I could see how God created in me a need to help everyone I could. I cannot stress enough how this was a turning point in my life. I started being pulled by a vision and could feel the hand of someone much bigger than myself beginning to guide my steps toward a future of purpose and fulfillment through helping others.

## Seeds of Joy

Remember the first time you fell in love? You just could not get that person out of your mind. You thought of them all the time, and it was effortless. No one made you think about them, yet you find yourself wanting to spend every possible second with them. This is how I felt when I first started falling in love with the idea of helping the impoverished kids I was reading about in my magazines.

I thought about them often, scheming in my own mind ways I could help. I remember days where I would spend the afternoon cutting out pictures of impoverished children and pasting them on my bedroom wall. I was dreaming, and I was dreaming big. I almost felt like I was dreaming for them. These children knew only suffering, hunger, and pain. All I could think about was how I was going to help these kids; somehow, someday, I was going to help them have a better life.

The more I thought about them, the more intense my desire to help became. Images in *National Geographic* became deeply imbedded in my heart. Even though my parents did not support my intentions to help these children, I could not justify getting mad or sad about anything because I at least had food in my belly and a roof over my head. Though I didn't yet understand the intellectual meaning of compassion, the spirit of the word was living in me.

🦋

Just like the butterfly, I too

awaken in my own time.

— Deborah Chaskin

# 2

## Gratefully Paralyzed

**AS A CHILD,** there was no excuse for sickness of any kind.  It
was only when my sickness was to the point of being unbearable
that I even thought about mentioning anything health-related to
my parents.  I often had common colds that no one in our home
noticed, and less often were the times I needed medical attention.
One day, however, I needed major medical attention.

It was a cold day during the fall of 1969, and I had been feeling
terribly sick for days.  Following the typical family protocol my
father set, I made little mention of it at home, and no one knew just
how sick I was until that school day.  I remember trying to make it
through the day, my knees weak and my entire body shaking.  My
teacher realized I was very ill, and she was deeply concerned when
I mentioned my parents knew about my health but sent me to
school anyway.  Even when my teacher called my parents, my father
brushed it off to the side, not wanting to deal with it.

After much persuasion, my teacher convinced my father I needed immediate medical attention, and I was taken to a doctor right away. All I wanted to do was go straight home to bed, but the doctors were franticly trying to figure out why I was so sick. They were looking for explanations as to how my health ended up at this point. I felt like they were never going to stop asking me questions.

Then they started the tests and examinations. The medical teams began with blood samples, and the tests went on and on for what seemed like weeks. My temperature was extremely high, and the doctors seemed very concerned. I was so confused and worried. All I knew for sure was I felt terrible and completely exhausted. The doctor had advised my parents I needed more extensive medical attention, and he recommended I be taken to a hospital.

After another day and night of tests at the hospital, they diagnosed me with rheumatic fever that had progressed into kidney damage. This was all a result of strep throat that had not been medically treated for weeks.

I was immediately admitted to the hospital and assigned a room. Before I hit the twenty-four hour mark of my hospital stay, my skin tone started turning purple. This obviously sent a major red flag, and several doctors began studying me all over again. I spent all my waking moments taking test after test after test.

After several days, they informed my family that my left kidney was completely diseased and needed to be removed. Keep in mind, this was back in 1969, and kidney transplants did not have very high success rates. But, I needed one immediately.

The first step was a biopsy of my kidney. When I woke up from the procedure, I could not feel my legs. This was not only alarming to the doctors, my family, and me, but it was also unexplainably terrifying. To not have feeling in your legs is indescribable, but in all the validated panic of the moment, I could still hear God whisper to my soul that all was well, and I had much for which to be grateful. I listened to that voice amidst the horror, and I still believe that voice to this very day. No matter in what situation we find ourselves, there is always someone facing a worse circumstance.

Every day they would take more tests, and every day the test results did not look positive. Absolutely everyone seemed concerned but me. Through it all, I remembered there was always someone suffering more than me. Was this perhaps the secret to enduring pain? It would take me years to learn that it was.

## Joy In Pain

One day I asked the nurse if I could go down to the Burn Unit to visit the children. She looked puzzled to say the least. Even though my legs were numb, I could still feel my spirit pushing me forward. The mantra of my life and the goal of each day was to find joy in my pain.

During my three-month stay at the hospital, I had over seventeen roommates, and all but seven passed away. Every day I was given, I gained strength by not giving a single thought to being a victim of suffering. I couldn't articulate that resolve at age ten, but I knew for sure I wasn't going to feel sorry for myself.

By the age of ten, I had seen so much suffering that I resolved to help each one of my roommates through their pain and trauma. I recall a young girl who was not allowed to have any food and was kept alive by an IV. When the nurse had left the room, she asked for some M&M's. I snuck out of bed, crawled into my wheelchair, and pushed myself over to her bedside. The smile she had on her face is with me to this day, and I'll never forget the joy she received from those few pieces of candy.

Where did I get the strength? Was it from the Divine? I truly believe so. Whatever or wherever it came from, it is still with me to this very day.

## Expect the Miraculous

At this point, all my parents could do was pray. They called everyone they knew to continue to pray for my healing.

It wasn't until after I spent almost an entire school year in the hospital that I began to regain the feeling in my legs. There was no particular rhyme or reason as to why I regained feeling. I didn't try to intellectually rationalize what happened; I just embraced and appreciated it. You cannot logically explain matters of the heart; you can only take them in and enjoy them. I began therapy immediately, and it didn't take my legs long to remember what they do best! I was walking in no time! The medical records eventually recorded these events as a "miraculous healing".

If you find yourself standing before a magnificent painting and you try to intellectually assess and explain the painting, you miss the beauty. Beauty cannot be explained; it can only be taken in and appreciated. I certainly see this as a miraculous healing and I don't need any further explanation.

I am thankful today that I had this experience, as it strengthened my gift of empathy, care, love, and compassion for all those who suffer. I believe with my whole heart that if we reach outside of our own suffering, no matter what that might be, we would realize there are many suffering more than ourselves.

We tend to think only about ourselves when going through

painful circumstances, and this is your story speaking to you instead of you speaking to your story. For me, finding the seeds in adversity was a very rewarding and fulfilling effort (and I will tell you, it is an effort, just like planting crops). You wait to see how those seeds will grow. You will eventually see the results; I certainly have. This was the beginning of my journey of compassion and re-writing my story!

## Your Butterfly

I share intimate details of my life story with you because I've been through, what it felt like at times, was hell and back. I didn't just wake up one day with a silver spoon in my mouth and start eating golden sprinkled frosted flakes! I've been through amazing times and terrible times. I want to share this with you because I know you've been through difficult times, too. Perhaps they are times you want to forget. But just remember, you can re-write your life story and begin again fresh and new. You can find that spark within that will help you transcend your current circumstances. You can find your inner butterfly, break out of your cocoon, and fly!

## Your First Wing

The first wing of your butterfly is your story of inspiration. We all have an inner story of what inspires us that was written on our soul before we were even born. Our job is to sift through a few questions in order to find inspiration. All you need to do, in order to discover what truly inspires you, is to ask the right questions to the right person.

There are thousands of books written on how to discover your purpose in life and how to discover what inspires you. You could spend days upon weeks reading, when the real truth is that in order to understand who you are and what inspires you, you must first understand who God is and what He has done for you.

Then you must begin asking the right questions. I am really hitting on this right now because many people tell me they have been thinking about what their life purpose is for so many years and they don't have the answers yet. Many people worry about what their purpose is or what inspires them, but they don't truly think about what their purpose is in a way that is intentional. There is a major difference between worrying and thinking.

When we live inspired, we are constantly moving forward. Without inspired work, the work is not worth doing, and we can be in a self-imposed rut. Working or living uninspired will always make you feel stuck, and no matter how you put it, being stuck stinks.

Inspiration is such a key element to making life beautiful, but in order to discover our source of inspiration, we must discover the story of inspiration God placed in our heart. So, let's talk about the first piece of your personal butterfly wing: Inspiration. How you can discover what inspires you?

Your first step is to start paying attention to what makes you tick. You may be working at a job you hate. You could be in a marriage you don't like. Maybe you woke up one morning to find the person looking back at you in the mirror is someone who is all grown up but never became anything close to the person they set out to be. Wherever you may be, you can find inspiration when you begin to look. And you will also find a surprisingly pleasant secret: inspiration is looking for you, too. Notice what you look forward to.  What makes you come alive?  What gives you butter-flies?  We live in and notice these feelings day and night when we are children, but as we grow up, we rationalize these feelings as day-dreams or fantasies and nothing more.  Start giving serious thought as to what excites you.  What kinds of books and magazines do you truly enjoy reading?  What types of people intrigue you, and with whom do you enjoy visiting?  What interests and projects are you drawn to in your spare time?  What does your intuition urge you to explore or experience?  If it is a person, what is it about them that inspires you?  Are they doing something that you see yourself doing?  To truly be inspired, one must remove all jealousy of other people's belongings and experiences.  Jealousy and envy can no longer be a part of your life if you want to be inspired and in turn, inspire others.  When you start to uncover what inspires you, you must hold true to it.  There will be others in your life who will try to impose their own limitations upon you and cast shadows upon your abilities.  I have shared a few of those moments from my life, and you will have similar moments as well.

When someone suggests you can't do something, just remember they are only giving you their opinion.  While it is true everyone is entitled to their own opinion, that doesn't mean you have to listen to that person or take them to heart.  Remember, their opinion is probably an educated guess at best.  Many people, when giving you their opinion, will simply talk until they think they are making sense.  Most likely they are speaking to you out of their own pain.  They are doing their best to protect you and themselves from being hurt.  So, don't lose heart when someone tells you that you can't.

At this point you will face head-on one of the biggest roadblocks to an inspirational life: being someone of whom others approve. We try to make everyone happy, please people, and be perfect in their eyes. We forget we are already perfect in God's eyes. We find ourselves saying yes when we mean no. It is only a matter of time before this kind of attitude turns into resentment. You can become resentful towards yourself and others whom you've allowed to sway you off course. Resentment eventually leads to anger, which leads to unforgiveness. The only way to avoid resentment is to have the courage to be imperfect. Your life depends on you affirming the following to yourself:

*I am enough*

*This is who I am*

*I am beautiful*

*I am talented*

*I am...*

Remain internally confident and externally humble.

Your resilience and commitment to living this new inspired life is often tested and formed during hard times. The absolute best ingredient to becoming resilient is to manage your emotions when bad things happen.

Pause. Breathe. Gain perspective.

When something bad happens to me, I try to compare it

to other circumstances much worse than my own. To create a habit of resilience, you must always ask, "How can I gain from this?" Life's hard times can teach you many things. Lessons don't always happen right away, but if you keep looking, you'll find them and an inspired life. To begin discovering this wing of your butterfly, use this space in the book to journal your responses to the questions I posed. Keep this book with you at all times so when inspiration comes, you can easily write down your thoughts before they slip away.

*What makes you come alive?*

*List some of your favorite songs. What do their lyrics speak to you?*

*When did you experience tears of inspiration? What was happening? Who was involved with this experience?*

We delight in the beauty of the butterfly, but rarely admit the changes it has gone through to achieve that beauty.

- Author Unknown

# 3

## Deathbed Forgiveness

**WAS I ANGRY** at what happened to me? Did I blame my parents for not caring enough to take me in to the doctor when I was sick? I never recall ever getting upset at anyone or any circumstance. I was still a little girl, and I still had my innocence. I really thought (in a beautiful naivety that I long to keep in my life) that the entire health ordeal was a good challenge for myself. Perhaps it was a game, and I was winning. Was this just a way to justify or cover up what I was really feeling? Maybe, but I strongly believe if I had become a victim of my own suffering, I would not have had the opportunity to reach out to others who were suffering more than me. Being empowered to go beyond the pain brought me JOY!

It was a challenge being raised by a father that seldom allowed us to show any emotions (happy or sad). On the other hand, it forced me to find joy in all things. Anytime I felt sad as a child, I

would think about others whose life circumstances were significantly worse than being trapped on a Minnesota hobby farm.

I made it a habit to always ask what it is that would make me so
sad. What could possibly be that bad that I would cry or stay angry
anyway? So what if my father continued to tell me I was stupid and
that I wouldn't amount to anything or was belted for the small-
est mistake. When I found myself in a wheelchair at age ten, the
physical pain was much easier for me to bear in many ways than
the emotional pain. I believe that is why the traumatic experience
of being paralyzed allowed me to escape from what I was feeling
emotionally, making it much easier to bear the physical pain. Not
being angry with my father allowed me to feel compassion towards
others, despite his expectations of me.

After I recovered from my paralysis, my father offered no sym-
pathy for my experience. It was as if nothing ever happened, and
I was right back to work again. School was waiting, and I started
sixth grade. At one of the required parent teacher conferences, my
parents were told I spent most of my time in school making sure
everyone else was happy. "Karen seems to be everyone's cheerlead-
er," my teacher commented.

Due to my long absence, the teacher suggested my parents help
me concentrate on my studies only and forget about trying to help
others. This was seemingly obvious advice, but matters of the heart
are not always logical. Sometimes you have to do the opposite of
what you think and go with what you feel. My teacher reasoned
that if I stopped talking and trying to make other kids happy, I
could possibly be someone someday. BE SOMEONE? Was I not
already someone?

It seemed like my father made it his mission to make sure I

believed I would never become anything or anyone special. You see, I believe even at this age, I did not want to follow other people's beliefs, ideas and opinions on how I should live my life. If I made other people happy, I actually became happy. This strategy was definitely working for me! I was able to overcome every crisis with this type of response: in seeking to make others happy, I received happiness as well. I would soon discover this is the only surefire way to be truly happy.

## Hurting People Hurt People

How can we overcome the criticism, lies, and beliefs of the influential people around us when we were young? What I eventually learned was that the lies those particular people told were not about me but about them. If we come to realize they are the ones who are suffering and the only thing they know how to do is make us suffer because of their pain, we can be compassionate toward them. They are simply doing the best they can with the understanding they have. I found out the long and hard way that what people see in others is a reflection of who they really are. Hurting people hurt people.

On my father's deathbed, years later, I asked him why he was so hard, critical, and mean to me. As he lay there dying, he replied in the most kind and gentle manner, "Karen, I was mean, critical, and demanding because I was weak, and you continued to show strength. The stronger you got through each blow, the angrier I got. You were much stronger than I was, but I could not tell you this. Instead, I put you down. What I wish I could have told you is that you were much stronger than I ever could be, that you were a hard worker, that you were special, and that I was so proud of you."

Tears rolled down my face as he shared these beautiful words.

I replied compassionately, "Dad, I am where I am today because of you. You taught me work ethic, you showed me organizational skills, you raised me to think like a man and not show emotion. I am successful today because of you, so therefore I want to thank you. I love you, Dad."

Through forgiveness, understanding, and appreciation for what he taught me rather than how he treated me, I was on my way to living a joyful life of compassion for people who are hurting. Since my father passed, I now look at everyone who hurts me as a person who is hurting deep inside; if I can endure the hurt, perhaps they will see that they need to heal and forgive those who have hurt them.

Compassion for the brokenhearted: first, last, and always!

## Your Second Wing

Now we come to the second wing of your inner butterfly. I shared my story with you that brought me, without knowing it, right to my second wing. This wing represents your past experiences. By past experiences, I mean any major moments in your life that you recognize, through reflection that molded you into the person you are today. These experiences can be both positive and negative. In fact, it is typically the worst moments of our lives that build the strongest character within us.

As you reflect on these moments, you will start to realize why you may respond in a certain way to specific events that happen. Why do certain songs bring tears to your eyes? Why does your heart break for the less fortunate in your community?

Your past experiences have forged your character and have made you who you are. In order to fully understand where we are called to go in the future, it often helps to observe our past. Pull what you want from it, and leave behind the rest.

## Hold onto Hope

As you look back on your past and think towards your future, I want you to know there is always hope. Never lose sight of hope.

If we can keep an attitude of gratitude for all we have been through, we can remember to have hope for our future. Truly joyful people are grateful for the things that most people take for granted. Those very people are focused on the big picture – the life for which God has created them.

> *I know what I'm doing. I have it all planned out – plans to take care of you, not abandon you, plans to give you the future you hope for.*
>
> Jeremiah 29:11 (The Message)

You are not your story. Your life is not what you thought it was. You are a hero in a much bigger story. You were put here for a very specific purpose, and that purpose will be revealed to you as you keep looking.

*What are some of your best past experiences that have shaped you?*

_____

_____

_____

*What are some of your past experiences that, although they were painful, shaped you as well?*

_____

_____

_____

*How could you help or support others going through similar experiences?*

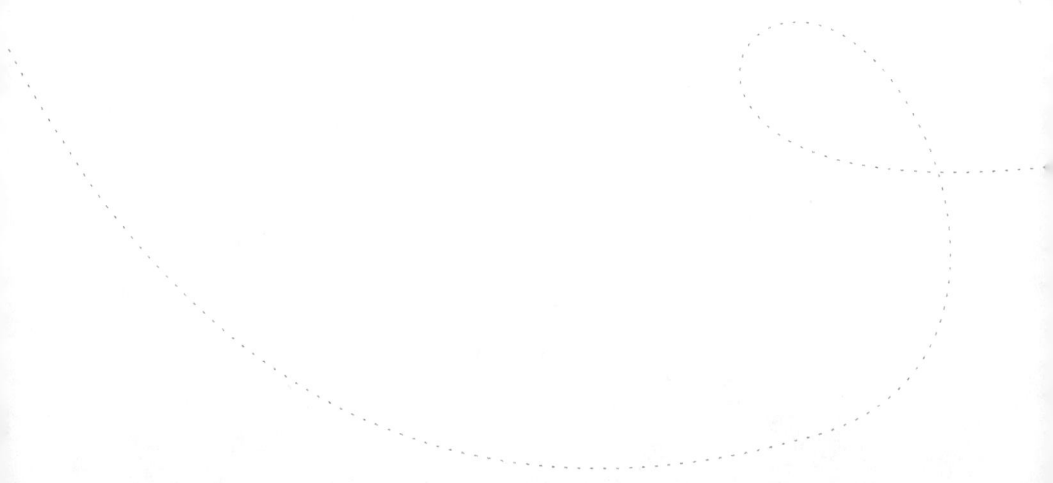

_____

_____

_____

Your life is like a Butterfly; it has
to go through changes before it
becomes beautiful.

- Author Unknown

# 4

## Carry Your Candle

**HIGH SCHOOL WAS** just not my cup of tea. In other words, high school was a drag. I mean a drag race. I was not your typical teenage girl who was on the cheerleading team, but quite the opposite. Being a tomboy was working for me as I felt I could protect myself from getting hurt. I was taught that girls are sissies and boys are bullies. This teaching significantly influenced my worldview.

As noted in an earlier chapter, my father raised me as a boy. I had no clue what it was to put a dress on and flirt with the boys, so I stuck with what I knew best. By this time, like any teenage boy, I had a fascination with muscle cars (my first car was a 1968 Ford Mustang with a 440 four-barrel engine). I spent a lot of time before school learning how to do 360s in the parking lot. If I was forced to play a girl's sport, I chose to become the team manager rather than being one of the players on the team. In doing this, I did not have to partake in any jealousy or girl talk. Girls were emotional. Boys were tough and did not cry. I embraced this masculine trait without realizing it would be a positive in the career choice I made as an adult.

Even though I didn't have a boyfriend, my parents wanted to ensure I never became pregnant during high school. They decided it was best I spend my time in church and suggested I become involved in a youth group. The church I attended for Wednesday night youth group was in downtown Minneapolis. On one particular night, I noticed a young girl outside the window on a very busy street. She must have been fourteen. She was pacing up and down, a cigarette in one hand and a backpack in the other. A million questions raced through my mind as I thought to myself, "What is she doing? Where are her parents? (Where were mine?) Why is she out there?"

I decided to excuse myself and tell my Youth Pastor I needed to go to the bathroom. I immediately dashed out the door and slowly approached this girl who was only about a year or two younger than me. I remember asking the girl her name.

She replied in a soft voice, "Erika."

I asked her where she was from. Shaking, she replied, "Up north." I asked, "Duluth?"

She said somewhere close to that. I then went way out on the limb (I dared myself) and asked her what on God's green earth she was doing standing along a sidewalk in downtown Minneapolis at 8:30 on a Wednesday night? She shared with me she had just run away from home and that she was out of money. She told me she was trying to see if she could turn a trick or two, and then she would be all right.

I replied, "What do you mean all right? What are you going to do to survive? Where are you going to live?" Upon hearing my questions, she started to cry. I immediately told her she could come home with me, and in the morning I would drive her three hours north back home where she belonged. So, instead of going back inside to youth group, I took her back to my home.

Upon my arrival, my father asked me, "Who the hell is this?" I tried to explain, but he interrupted me with, "Karen, why are you always trying to save the world. This is a young teenager who ran away from home. There is nothing you can do."

I informed my father she had no place to go, and that if I had not taken her home with me, she would have sold herself. He then warned me that this was the first and last time I could bring anyone home. Although I followed his order and took her home in the morning, this was just the start of my next journey. I started to carry my candle wherever it was needed to light someone else's path. It seemed odd, but this is the only thing that brought me joy.

When I returned to school, I heard the normal drama of high school break ups and people getting drunk at parties, and I thought to myself, "Now what is so exciting about that?" So every chance I had, I went back to the streets to find as many girls as I could. This continued for as long as I could get away with it without my father knowing. I was getting by with it. My father eventually had no other choice then to ignore and distance himself from me. Even though I was still living at home, at age sixteen I felt like I was on my own, and I was determined to light the path for anyone in need, regardless of who they were.

## Compassion in Action

Your third wing involves carrying your candle and identifying the activities or hobbies that express and bring forth compassion for others. These are things you may never have thought you would ever do but there was something inside you that just kept making you take another step. Just help one more person, just one more act of service.

It's beautiful. These activities can end up being a lot of work, just like mine did when I was helping those young women. It involved a lot of work and a lot of sleepless nights, but I didn't feel like I was working. I also never suspected I would be in the middle of the city, sneaking out to rescue prostitutes. How did this happen? I don't know except to believe it was the hand of God.

The ways to put your compassion into action find you; you don't find them. As you seek out a better life, these compassionate activities (your third butterfly wing) are actually seeking you.

I often find that people feel totally rescued when they find their third wing. When they discover a way to put their compassion into action, it is an unexplainable occurrence. It will sound totally strange until you experience this for yourself or truly listen to the stories of others.

Compassionate hobbies bring us back to what really matters, and that is the heart of others. You see, compassionate hobbies are not about achieving anything or about how many people you help; they are about matters of the heart. You are helping God rescue the heart of another. You will find yourself drawn to certain people, certain events, or certain circumstances. You were meant to find these people, and they were meant to find you. You are discovering your role in a much bigger story.

*But God will not take away life, and he devises means so that the*
*banished one will not remain an outcast.*

*2 Samuel 14:14*

Think about this ancient scripture. God devises plans and
means to rescue you, to rescue everyone. It is through your
compassion in action that you will first see a glimpse of this for
others and for yourself.

Your compassionate hobby takes advantage of and lever-
ages things at which you are naturally talented. More often than
not, you tend to de-value the things at which you are naturally
gifted. The things with which we are most familiar, we tend to
take for granted. But truly contemplate this: you were created in
an exact way for an exact purpose. Those skills and talents you
naturally possess are significantly valuable to you and to others.
Oh yes, you have a strength, and your strength is needed in the
world. Pay attention to these things my friend. Pay close attention, and never lose sight of the fact you were created with an
exact idea in mind.

Think of the world's most skilled inventors. The more skilled
the inventor, the better inventions they make, and the more precise
inventions with precise purposes. Well, you are an invention by
the greatest inventor in the entire universe. Pretty cool, huh! And
what does this say about YOU!?

This understanding demands our attention and our thoughts.
Think about what all this means, and start to connect some dots.

Isn't this cool! Now, as you have already started to notice, there
will be a central theme emerging from each of your butterfly wings.
Start to circle all the skills or experiences that have something

similar to them.

Can you see the pattern emerging even now? Doesn't this excite you!?

*What is pulling on your heart?*

_____

_____

_____

*Who is pulling on your heart?*

_____

_____

_____

*Where do you feel called to serve?*

_____

_____

_____

Beautiful and graceful, varied and enchanting, small but approachable, butterflies lead you to the sunny side of life. And everyone deserves a little sunshine.

— Jeffrey Glassberg

# 5

## Living Larger Than Your Fears

**I GREW UP FAST** and naturally became quite independent. As soon as high school ended, I was off to college. I went as far away as I could from my father's constant demands and expectations – California!

My freshman year is when I finally discovered I was no longer a tomboy and didn't have to be a tomboy anymore. I actually found a boy in whom I was interested. Scary! I was totally out of my comfort zone. At this point in time, it was safe to say I was a newbie to the dating scene. I had never before had a steady boyfriend. Of course, I did kiss a guy in 8th grade on the school bus, but afterwards everyone laughed at me. Why would this time be any different?

This nice, cute Christian boy from San Diego was a son of a doctor and a football player. My father would be so proud...or would he? I started to accept the belief that my father would not be proud of me, no matter what I did or didn't do. I decided I had to accept that I would never gain my father's approval. I could date Jesus, and he still would find things to complain about!

Even as I entertained the idea of dating this young stud, all kinds of questions ran through my mind. Do I tell this cute boy what I had been doing long before I arrived at college? Do I tell him I rescued prostitutes? Would he think I was crazy? He would likely never take me home to see his parents. Deep down, I still desired my father's approval, and one of the ways I was trying to gain that approval was through this young man's parents. If I could only get them to see I was a good person, with good intentions, I would actually feel that I mattered. I yearned for anyone that might notice that I was someone, that I was special.

This was the first time in my life that I felt alone. All alone with myself. I found myself wrestling with what had come to be the biggest question in my life: "Who am I?" Since I spent the first eighteen years of my life thinking of others and empathizing with other people's pain, I was now totally out of my comfort zone. Now the pain I had been harboring all these years started coming to the surface, and I had nowhere to run.

The more and more I thought about dating this guy, the more insecure and fearful I became. Looking back, I can see how the doubts I had about myself surfacing as I contemplated having a relationship in which I would need to do something I had never done before: talk about me, share my true self with someone, express my personality, and discuss my true passions. Some of you girls know what I am talking about; this is scary!

I really liked this guy, but I didn't know what to do. Should I start putting on a little lip-gloss and mascara like all the other girls?

What should I wear?  How should I act?  I was scared.  For the first time, I felt weak and vulnerable.  You see, this was all new to me.  At 16 years of age I was strong, bold, and daring.  Now, at 18, what was happening to me?

I had to decide to live larger than what scared me, for this cute boy and for the rest of my life.  As I look back now and reflect, I understand what happened.  I went beyond my comfort zone.  I did not know what to do if I was not thinking or helping others.  It was an empty feeling.

One Saturday afternoon, this handsome guy with whom I was infatuated, decided to teach me how to play frisbee.  I did not want to let him in on my secret that I was a great frisbee player, so I decided to fake it.  I was feeding his cute little ego and letting him teach me.  Then it happened; one of the cars in the school parking lot stalled.  The girl got out of her car, all flustered and glittered.  I immediately went over and asked her to pop the hood.  It's safe to say she was confused why I asked while my frisbee trainer was intimidated.  I reassured her and asked for a quick look.  After a few minutes of pulling here and there, I discovered she had a bad solenoid.  I jiggled it enough to get her car started again, and they couldn't believe it.  I directed her to take it to the nearest shop and told her exactly what she needed to tell them to get her car running again.

My prospective first boyfriend was beside himself and seemed totally taken aback.  He asked me how I knew what was wrong with her car.  I just commented that it was magic, and I got lucky this time.  I didn't want to tell him the truth.  I was afraid of who I was, and he was becoming afraid of me, too.

For the first time in my life I wanted to be a normal girl.  I wanted more than anything to be a young woman, to cry and have girlfriends I could talk to. But what would I talk to them about? I didn't have typical girl problems. I had never dated and didn't know what breaking up was all about. I didn't spend an hour getting ready or take the time to read the most recent issue of Vogue. What was I getting myself into, and why was I feeling this way?

After the first week of my freshman year, this cute boy and I officially became an item. I was scared to tell him I had never intimately kissed a boy. For fear of scaring him off, I could not tell him I spent my teenage years working my ass off, and in my spare time, racing cars and rescuing prostitutes. It's fair to say I was getting in touch with my feminine heart and discovering it as I went along. I was nervous, to say the least, about making myself vulnerable to him and giving away a piece of me I had never before shared – my femininity.

Well, I quickly began to find out the strange phenomena that cute, nice and charming boys were more promiscuous than most. He had a nice apartment dorm on campus, and while I decided to spend the night, I planned to tell him it was too early in the relationship to have sex. Truth be told, I was scared. He respected my wishes, and we stayed up all night talking about his failed relationships and God. As for me, I had nothing to share but my adventures of prostitutes and fast cars. I had no prior relationship experience, so I just decided to listen. It's funny how good we become at getting other people to talk about themselves when we are too scared to share ourselves with them.

In the morning, he kindly asked if I would make French toast, bacon, and eggs. Um, what? Are you kidding me? I had never even been in a kitchen, let alone made an egg. I had no idea what to do.

I immediately called and woke my roommate up at 8 A.M. on a Saturday morning and asked her how to make French toast. Well, what would most college co-eds think if their roommate called them at 8 A.M. after being out all night on a date to then ask how to make him breakfast? She didn't want to talk about breakfast; she wanted to hear about sex! I proudly told her I didn't give into temptation, to which she responded, "You are not going to make French toast for a guy you prayed with! Are you kidding?!" Eventually, my first crush found a new girl. Was I mad? Not really, but I was a little heartbroken. The only way to assuage my heart was to get right back to helping others.

## Back At It!

I did not waste any time; compassion was in my blood! Every time I felt pain coming, I would try to numb that feeling as quickly as possible. So, I exchanged Saturday morning French toast for a phone bank! I applied to be a phone counselor at World Vision International. I would take calls from people who desired to sponsor a child in a developing country. This was right up my alley!

Once again, instead of getting mad that my first crush found a new girl, I decided to go back to what brought me joy! Compassion: first, last, and always!

When I allowed compassion to be at the forefront of my life, it healed my broken heart.

## Next Semester

As I began the second semester of college, I started despising school. I viewed it as just another thing I needed to do to gain my father's approval. My job at World Vision was my real university. I took part of my paycheck and paid the smart students to do my papers so I could do what I felt compelled to do: make a difference in the lives of children less fortunate than me. I never told my parents that I rarely went to class. My heart was in a completely different place, and silently I honored that.

What I really wanted my dad to know was that I was a good girl, that I was going where my heart led me, and I was serving as a light in someone else's life. If my father only knew that I was a good girl, I thought, then he could be really proud of me. While that eventually happened shortly before he died, I waited for over 35 years to feel his pride.

## A Sign of Things to Come

During the winter months in mountainous San Bernardino, California, we were blessed with snow. Coming from Minnesota, I wanted to stay as far away as possible from the snow, but my college friends found it fun to go up to the mountains and enjoy the snow. I, on the other hand, would stay back and curl up inside. One day, while the others were in the mountains, I posted a simple ad in a local newspaper that read, "Music student will sing at your special occasion/wedding at a moment's notice. Can sing just about anything!"

The next weekend I received a call that someone was in dire need of someone to sing "You Light Up My Life" at a wedding in Robert Schuller's incredible Crystal Cathedral near San Diego. The scheduled singer had come down with laryngitis. I never gave it another thought and just did it! I needed additional funds to pay the other students to do my papers so I could work at World Vision. So, I borrowed a classmate's car and I went and sang their desired song without even rehearsing.

I remember the only way I made it through the wedding was to visualize what those little children in developing countries were singing when they received sponsorship from World Vision. Those little voices singing, "You light up my life, you give me hope...to carry on." I didn't realize it, but this level of sacrifice and ingenuity to give was my heart growing more and more toward my current mission as an auctioneer.

✷

Butterflies so still, behind a pane
of glass. Exhibition of beauty or
travesty. Though beauty is seen,
beauty is not felt. It is the pain
behind the glass I see.

- Andrew Hawkins

# 6

# Don't Get Mad, Get Blessed

**EVENTUALLY,** my wonderful adventure in California led me back to Minnesota. I brought back some incredible lessons learned from my many challenges. I was so excited to share my experiences, but I was unable to share anything about my endeavors and the woman I had become with my parents. I understood I would only be the subject of more criticism. I believed that no matter what I shared with them, it seemed they could never be proud of me.

Moving back home with my parents, I was lucky to find a job and eventually a husband, the only man that met my father's approval. I remember my father emphatically telling me not to screw up the relationship because I would never do any better. During the relationship, I often thought of my Ramon back in California. You see, before coming back to Minnesota, I was smitten with a Los Angeles police officer that I met while attending church. Ramon was a dark and handsome Mexican man. He came from a huge family that was very close, and I wanted nothing more than to be accepted. His family did just that. Even though our relationship was far from perfect, I still had strong feelings for this man. How could I ever inform my father I was having a relationship with a Mexican cop from L.A.? So, I did the one thing I strongly suggest not doing throughout this book. I made a major life decision, not according to the story I wanted to create for my life, but for the story someone else wanted for me. I married the man my father approved of instead of finding the man that I could possibly love and be married to forever.

The story of the marriage my father approved of eventually ended after nineteen years and two children. However, I am truly grateful for this because of the absolute joy and blessing it is to be the mother of these two children. In moving forward, my mantra was to find the blessings through the pain. My two magnificent children have taught me and revealed more to me about my true self than any other element of my entire life. I would never have found my wings if it were not for my children.

When my first child was born, motherhood was the first positive distraction from my interest in children around the world. I fully embraced being a mother and blossomed in this role. It brought me the joy I did not have in my marriage, and I eagerly looked forward to the birth of our second child two years later. We decided to choose biblical names for our children. Our son was named Matthew, and if our second-born was a girl, the plan was to name her Sarah.

Things changed when she was born totally blind. My water broke two weeks early, which caused an infection and ultimately blindness. Instead of feeling sorry for myself or becoming a victim, I decided to find some kind of blessing in this absolutely unfortunate situation. Meeting with much resistance, I suggested that if she were never to see again, that her name should be SUNNY!

And so it was, but not everyone in my life accepted the name graciously. My in-laws commented, "Is Karen serious? 'Sunny' is not a proper name. 'Sarah' would be more fitting." It is rare that others freely accept bold moves in our lives, especially as you begin to find your wings. You, too, will make bold moves that cause discomfort in people around you.

My husband and I eventually discovered that our daughter's blindness was merely a temporary problem caused by bacterial film across her eyes. Praise God, her blindness lasted only a few days and her name remains the same today – Sunny.

## Almost Defeated

Now that I had children of my own, my father made every effort to tell me I was not a good mother. He reminded me if my kids grew up to be trouble, it would be my fault. How was I supposed to find a way out of this? His criticism finally started to take control of me.

Soon after Sunny was born, I started putting on weight. For the first time, I allowed my father's negativity to make me feel like a nobody. My story took a turn for the worse; I was becoming a victim. My husband became even more distant, and I never felt accepted or loved for who I was. I remember every day putting the kids in their car seats and driving to Baskin Robbins to buy ice cream. I found comfort from my empty marriage and the lack of my father's love in ice cream. Why could I not find the blessings anymore?

Where did my positive attitude go? Where was the empowering light that once existed inside me? What happened to the voice that reminded me of others facing worse circumstances and gave me the strength to keep holding on for a second longer? Why was I, for the first time, becoming defeated? I felt so alone in my pain and emptiness. I became angry with myself for losing the strength that carried me through more than twenty years of my life. What could be so bad that I would lose my self-worth and became a victim drowning my pain in quarts of ice cream? I would go down in the basement and weep while putting toys back in their bins. I cried out to God, asking him why I was so weak, why I was so alone, and why I hurt so much?

My ultimate solution to everything, which was helping others, stopped working. I did not feel the joy anymore. How could I find the joy in putting on weight and feeling like I didn't even matter? There was no joy in being overweight. There was no joy in my marriage. How could I get it back?

One day, the light bulb came on. Perhaps God sent one of His Angels. I realized that the only way for me to find the joy again was to take down the biggest barrier I had created in my story; the barrier of not forgiving my father. My resentment toward him was like a fortified wall of bronze that separated me from my joy. I decided the only way to get back my joy was to forgive my father.

Forgive my father? How could I? The only way was to realize hurting people hurt people. My father was doing the best he could with the understanding he had. It frustrated him that, despite his lack of approval and critical spirit, I carried on and made the best of it while he was miserable and stuck in his own pain with no way out. I couldn't let resentment win. This feeling or my father was not going to get me to the point where I felt sorry for myself. Indeed, this needed to be the time to forgive him for all the criticism.

By the time I realized this, I had tipped the scale at 210 pounds. I was angry I had allowed my father's criticism and my husband's lack of interest in me to take me to a place of self-defeat. So, I made an irrevocable decision to draw motivation from a higher purpose and used that motivation to lose weight as the first step in getting back my wings. Even though it would be difficult to regain my compassionate heart, my desire to make a difference and carry the candle into someone else's darkness while going through my own darkness was what I decided to do. In doing this, I discovered the solution to finding joy in life, no matter what. Be the light for others, and yours will shine in ways you forgot it could. In moving forward, there have been many more instances where I felt I was becoming defeated, but I just needed to keep my candle lit and never allow another to blow it out.

✴

I embrace emerging experience.
I participate in discovery. I am
a butterfly. I am a butterfly
collector. I want the experience
of the butterfly.

- William Stafford

# 7

# Teaching Compassion

**NO MATTER HOW** hard I had to look, finding the blessings
in every difficult situation robbed anger of its power; it could no
longer steal my joy. If my joy was gone, I continued to think of different ways I could be a blessing to others. The funny part is, when
we look for something, we find it. All our questions and prayers
get answered, even if sometimes not in the way we expect. If I
stumbled into self-pity, I would immediately throw my heart and
mind into the question of how I could bless those around me. This
became my ultimate anti-depressant.

I remember a time when I took Matt and Sunny to rent a movie.
My son was about eight, and his inability to make a decision was
trying my patience. I told him if he didn't pick out a movie in less
than a minute, I would make sure he was thankful he even got the
chance to pick out a movie. After a minute and still no movie,
I loaded my kids into the minivan and drove them to an area in

Minneapolis where kids their age did not have T.V's, let alone the privilege of a movie rental.

When we reached the right neighborhood, I opened up the door and asked both Matt and Sunny to get out. They kept saying. "Mom, what are you doing?" I simply explained I wanted them to realize how fortunate they were. I wanted them to meet kids who would be grateful for the chance to watch TV; these were kids who could only dream of picking out and renting a movie.

In less than a minute, a dozen African American kids ranging in age from eight to fifteen surrounded Matt and Sunny. They started in with a, "Yo, what's up, dude? What's your mama dropping you in our neighborhood for?"

All Matt could respond with was a short and hesitant, "I took too long to pick out a movie." Sunny did not say a thing as she held tight to her brother's sleeve. It's safe to say that a few minutes of conversation between these kids and my very deer-in-the-headlight kids made a significant impression. I asked if they had learned a lesson, but they didn't answer. They never had to answer me. I knew they understood.

I was determined as a mother to teach my children to be thankful for everything they had. We have to consciously remember, three-quarters of this world wakes up every day without food or water. It is so easy and seductive to take for granted all we have. The most loving people I've ever met have profound appreciation for the simple things most of us take for granted.

## Shiny Shoes

One weekend, our family decided to take the train and spend a day in Chicago on Michigan Avenue to see the sights. We rode in a horse drawn carriage, visited an F.A.O. Swartz Toy Store, and toured museums and the famous Pier on Lake Michigan. What a lovely day!

As we walked directly along the city park bordering Michigan Avenue, our kids for the first time witnessed the many homeless bums strewn across the empty park benches. I seized the opportunity to impress upon my children's hearts how fortunate we were and that we should always be thankful for our blessings.

Later that day, my husband bought a new pair of shoes. He was now an executive at a consulting firm and felt he needed a new pair of shoes. Immediately after the purchase, the store clerk asked if we wanted the old shoes put in a box. My husband appeared puzzled as he asked, "In a box?" At this moment, I had an immediate vision of compassion. I was ecstatic about the idea of putting the shoes in a box and dropping them off at the city park where the homeless people would love a pair of shoes! I immediately shared this idea with Matt, Sunny, and their father. What was I thinking? Would I meet anything but opposition on this one? Then my son blurted out, "Yeah, Dad. Let's do it! It will be neat to see someone looking in the box and finding a pair of shoes. How cool would that be?"

So, with some resistance from my husband, we went to the park, put the shoebox under a bench, and waited. In a matter of minutes, a man came along and tried them on. They apparently didn't fit so he put them back. Then, wouldn't you know it, the next person that came along tried the shoes on, they fit, and he had a victory for the day!

What a beautiful lesson for the kids to see in action: in giving, we receive the greatest blessings. Compassion: first, last, and always!

## The Nature of Compassion

Compassion is pure emotion. Compassion is first and foremost, the ability to identify with another. When you can identify, you begin to understand that this person is searching for some kind of happiness in his or her life. This person has known sadness, loneliness, and despair and is seeking to fill his or her needs just like you. Try to find the similarities between you and this person because we all are learning about life. When you can share in someone else's suffering while acting on a desire to alleviate or reduce that suffering for their sake, you are exercising compassion and benefitting by taking the attention off yourself.

The hardest and most difficult compassion to show is in easing the suffering of those who have hurt or mistreated us. This did not come easy for me as it took years to find compassion for my father. Since writing this book, I have found the ability to feel compassion for the husband who, I felt, did not understand my heart.

Compassion allows you to imagine what kind of struggles or pain that have happened in order for that person to hurt you the way they did. By practicing this, you will understand that their action was not about you but about what they were going through. What a freeing and relieving understanding! Just by doing this, you will show others that one can truly be happier in life with a heart full of compassion for those who are suffering and those who indeed hurt us.

## Forgiveness

Along my path, I've thankfully had many opportunities to learn how to truly forgive. Forgiving may be a simple concept, but it certainly isn't easy. We all need help to do it. Without forgiveness, you are the prisoner, and the one who hurt or betrayed you is free. The only way to be free is through forgiveness, no matter how hard it is.

Below are five steps I hope will help you on the road to forgiveness.

First, make a mental list of those you have not forgiven and the reasons why. This will be a hard exercise, and you will have many opportunities to push it aside until tomorrow. I urge you to make the time, sit alone, pray for help, and get it done.

Then, recognize the source of the pain, and accept that your present situation is not a happy one. Realize that you are not alone and accept the fact that you can't control how the person who hurt you is feeling. What you can do is learn to forgive.

Next, remember that even good people sometimes make horrible mistakes. Even though what was done to you was horrible, that does not necessarily make the person horrible. Try separating the person from the behavior. This certainly can be very difficult. Spend some time thinking about the good qualities that he or she possess. I had to do this with my father. I dug deep down in my heart, and I just knew my father was a good man. He never meant to hurt me or verbally abuse me. One must realize that those who hurt you are hurting too. I have come to the understanding that so many people are unable to love another without first loving themselves.

Resolve to get all the anger out of your system once and for all. You need to release the pent up frustration inside you. Promise yourself that once you are done, you will feel much better. Pray for God to help and provide you with the grace to forgive. Give yourself some time to release the anger and the pain. Then, you can get started with the healing process.

Release the offender and yourself from pain. Forgiveness is 100% your responsibility. Even if the offender doesn't seem to care one way or another, you still need to forgive for your own sake. Holding a grudge will only make you feel worse, and you become imprisoned by your own anger. You live in the past with the anger, and you live in the future yearning for revenge.

Refuse to go back and instead move forward. This takes courage, true resilient courage. Let the person who harmed you know that you forgive him or her. Whether or not that person responds is something over which you have no control. The only thing you can control is your forgiveness. Once you are able to forgive not just the offender but yourself, you will finally be able to move on with your life.

I hope these steps will help you and relieve you of the heavy burden you have been carrying. Un-forgiveness blocks the flow of abundant blessings. Do we not all desire abundance? So what we are really saying is we desire forgiveness both to give it and receive it.

Your life is like a Butterfly; it has
to go through changes before it
becomes beautiful.

- Author Unknown

# 8

## Becoming a Compassionate Auctioneer

**DETERMINED TO** try to make my marriage work after losing all the weight I so selfishly gained, I felt the need to share my story with others. The only way to share my path of forgiveness and the story of finding blessings through my loneliness and pain was to share it with as many people as possible. I needed to build a platform.

A friend told me about a pageant for married women called Mrs. Minnesota. I told her I couldn't enter a pageant for married women when my marriage was failing. Upon hearing the climate of my marriage, she absolutely couldn't believe her ears. To her and many other people in my life, I was the perfect woman with the perfect family in front of the proverbial picket fence and all. When I set out for a goal, such as losing weight, I effortlessly reached it in their eyes. But this wasn't the case; it was in fact far from the truth.

The more I thought about running for the pageant, though, the more it made sense. No one knew my marriage was failing except my friend, so what did I have to lose?  With this title and platform, I could get myself in the door to speak about how to stay empowered and help others.  Who knew, maybe I could reach out to other wives with empty marriages and make a difference for them too!

The biggest challenge was I had barely ever watched Miss America because I was too busy watching Dukes of Hazard.  I was an unlikely candidate for a pageant.  I did not know how to wear high heel shoes or walk like a lady.  Add to this makeup, lipstick, and backcombed hair to match the sparkly gowns, and I was really getting out of my comfort zone!

## Trading in Overalls for an Evening Gown

I needed to quickly learn all of these things, so I decided to enroll myself in not only pageant etiquette classes, but also voice and performance coaching.  I did what I had to do, and I didn't give it a second thought.  If this is what I have to do to get my message out there on forgiveness and living a life of purpose, so be it.

I entered the pageant, and to my surprise, I won!  As Mrs. Minnesota, I went on to compete for Mrs. International.  I recall when I made it to the top ten, and my parents were in the audience.  I had to pick a question out of the bowl and answer it.  My question was, "If you wrote your own autobiography, what would be the title?"

Wow!  What kind of question was that?  While I was shaking profusely inside, I was able to remain calm on the outside by reminding myself of my ultimate desire in life: to make a difference.  I answered with, "Life Is an Echo: What you give out will come back to you.  What you sow, you eventually reap.  But the most difficult chapter to learn in the book of life is the fact that what you see in others also exists in you."  I would encourage everyone reading this book to find the best in every person you meet and find the best in every situation. Through this, you will find your greatest blessing.

The pageant experience was great, but I didn't win Mrs. International and thus infuriated my father. He felt that I didn't really answer the question and he was the first to remind me of that. The next day on the plane from Texas back to Minnesota, my father would not even sit with me on the plane. Not only that, he had to tell everyone around where he was seated that his daughter lost the Mrs. International crown because she didn't correctly answer her question. He called me a loser and that this trip was a waste of his time.

Did this hurt? Of course. But I refused to allow this to penetrate my heart and once again make me unable to get out of my pain and become a victim. At that moment, I actually felt sorry for my father. I did not even get upset because I was able to see the pain he had, which was much more than mine. I was destined and determined to find the joy! Many years later, it paid off.

## Growing Beyond Beauty

That first year as Mrs. Minnesota allowed me to stand in front of many women's groups to share my message of hope, forgiveness, and finding purpose through pain and struggles. It was an amazing year. Even after I gave up the title to my successor, I continued to speak to a variety of audiences.

Since I had forgiven my father, I was on my way to realizing that no matter what I did, I would never gain my father or husband's approval. I really wondered why I had wasted so much of my time trying to get these two men to love me and be proud of me. The more I reflected on this question, the more I realized what I needed to do: involve my father in my life more.

Realizing that my father was only mean, crabby, and critical because he was the one hurting, I thought about how to engage with him without becoming the subject of his criticism. To my amazement, the answer came rather quickly when my brother Loren called and suggested the three of us go to Auction School. Dad was retired, and he had nothing else to do, so perhaps this could be the perfect solution. My brother had a wild and crazy idea that we could open up an auction consignment house and be in business together.

Since I had overcome the issues with my father, I really believed this could actually work. As I began to entertain this thought, I went back to one of the only positive memories I had with my father during my childhood, which was when he brought me to my first auction. I was about six years old, and I can to this day remember being fascinated with the auctioneer. It was so exciting to me how fast he would talk and the excitement that would swirl through the crowds. All of a sudden, I started to recall how I secretly wanted to be like this man and do what he was doing! I loved the energy, the entertainment, and the thrill of the whole auction

To top it all off, the auctioneer proudly wore a huge belt buckle that was bigger than the platter on which we served Thanksgiving Dinner. If I could take these childhood memories into this new venture with my father and brother, perhaps it would be exactly what my father and I needed. Thus our journey together began and we attended auction school.

As we often do when we try to do something different, I ran into all kinds of self-doubt as to how I could actually be successful. I was required to learn so many things that I thought were completely irrelevant to my new profession as an auctioneer. I didn't comprehend why I needed to understand what diseases cows had and what year or era a piece of furniture came from.

This whole auctioneer thing was not what I envisioned. I loved the excitement, the energy, and the thrill of the auction. What I didn't like were the little details I needed to learn that seemed so far from what I came to learn. But as with any new skill we strive to learn or are forced to learn, we must be willing to do the daily grind, master the fundamentals, and do the work that other people are not willing to do in order to live a life most people never live. So I pushed forward, learning the nuances of being an auctioneer, and we made it! Auction school was a success, and we were grateful for having completed the education, but now we had to figure out what to do next!

When I returned my husband appeared unhappy with my ambitious goals and dreams. We would have had to borrow a lot of money to open up an auction house, and furthermore, it would take away too much of my time with Matt and Sunny. They were eight and ten at the time, and my main job was to be a mother. I continued to be thankful.

My father, on the other hand, seemed happier than I had ever seen him. He spent every waking moment perfecting his bid chant. My brother lived nine hours from us, so nothing worked out for him to get involved in a prospective family auction business.

## Challenges, Lessons, and Triumphs from Mistakes

A week after graduating from auction school, a newspaper reporter somehow found out that a former Mrs. Minnesota became an auctioneer. The truth of the matter was that I wasn't completely an auctioneer, nor did I really think I would ever be one. After the article was published, I received a call from a non-profit that was raising funds for diabetes. They asked if I would be interested in selling a few items at their charity golf tournament, and I didn't have anything to lose. Why not?!

Well, my first auction experience involved losing my cookies about two minutes before going on stage. The facts were getting in the way of my dream. I couldn't stop thinking about how I had never sold fine wine, art, a luxury trip, or a fur coat. These items were a far cry from what I learned to sell at auction school where we had to sell antiques, tractor seats, and feeder pigs by the pound. I had never experienced stage fright like this before in my life. The first item on auction was a fur coat. Making the most of this new experience, I started out by saying, "What a beautiful full length mink coat we have here for your bidding pleasure. Gentlemen, this would make a great Christmas gift for your wife."

My first words as a professional auctioneer resulted in silence. What did I say? What did I do wrong? Why was everyone quiet? Then, from the front table an older distinguished gentleman whispered, "Hanukah, not Christmas, Karen." At that moment I wanted to crawl under the table. I thought this would be my first and last auction.

Then came my saving grace: God and humor. I tried to think of something witty to say on the spot. So I came back with, "Ladies and gentlemen, it just dawned on me that I am the only Gentile in this room, so therefore I will refrain/digress and say to all of my Hebrew friends, Happy Hanukkah!" Most everyone applauded, and I went on to sell the coat!

Even though the auction was a success, I focused on all the things I didn't do well and wanted nothing more than to bury my head in the sand when I returned home. This is so easy for us to do, when we feel like we have made a huge mistake, and focus on the negative only.

After a few days, I received a call from someone who saw me at what I thought was my first and last auction. He remarked how entertaining I was and how I used humor to cover up my mistake. They went on to share that they sat on the board of another non-profit, and the organization would welcome the opportunity to use my skills for their upcoming auction. I met with them the next week to discuss the items and their financial goals. Within just two weeks of graduating from auction school, I was already selling again. With each passing auction, more calls came in from charitable organizations requesting my auctioneering skills. I thought to myself, "How wonderful is this? I can use this talent to assist non-profits in raising funds for those in need. Week after week, month after month, I would be making a difference."

I soon needed business cards and stationary. I shared my joy with my husband, and as with everything else I ever desired to do, if it did not make money, it went nowhere. All he said was my new adventure was costing money. I shared with him my belief that if someone is passionate about making a difference in people's lives and does something they love, money will perhaps eventually follow. He simply reminded me that I was involved in non-profits, and these organizations would not pay much for an auctioneer.

What is one to do when they don't receive any support, not even from their own family? I simply ignored the negativity and continued to volunteer my time. In a matter of a few months, I was volunteering at events where affluent people attended and wore very nice clothes. While I needed clothes, my husband was not too keen about me spending money to dress in a similar fashion as the guests at these fundraisers. How was I supposed to pay for clothes to do something for which I received no monetary compensation? That's when I decided to begin asking these organizations for just a little something for my time. The small amount of money for which I initially asked for was just enough to cover my dry cleaning and a professional up-do hairstyle.

Despite feeling my husband's lack of interest in my new adventure, I was determined to use this newfound talent to raise money for those less fortunate. I was living my purpose. I was back in my comfort zone.

I could not have been happier that these auctions were on weekends, which allowed me to continue my role as a mother, which I loved the most. When I could no longer keep up with the demand for my services, I drafted a simple contract based on a set fee for what the organization expected to raise plus additional compensation if I raised over their projections. With every auction, I was able to surpass the set fundraising goals. At this point, I felt I needed to raise my standard fee, which displeased a few organizations. They questioned why they should pay an auctioneer when a news anchor would provide the services for free. I responded, "They report the news and get paid; I should be paid something for my skills as an auctioneer."

One particular organization informed me that when they previously used a news anchor for an auction, they were able to raise

$50,000 more than when they used a volunteer. I then suggested to this prospective client that if I was unable to raise over $100,000, then they would owe me nothing for my time and talent.

They replied, "Karen, this is impossible! You will be doing this auction for no compensation," to which I responded, "If you will take some time to listen to a few suggestions I have to raise more funds, I think we can do this. I have some creative ideas and suggestions. Would you be willing to listen to them?" As it went, I raised $110,000 for this organization. This was my break. I went out on a limb, and the fruit was there. There were only so many Saturday and Sunday nights in a year, but the requests kept coming, and I kept raising my fee.

While the success of my auctioneering was scary at times, I was doing and going for what I felt was my purpose. If money followed, so be it. When I secured my first really big auction gig of 1,200 people, I was scared to death. I had never been up in front of an audience this big, but I was determined to succeed. I invited my father to come and see my work. He obliged, but on the way home, he commented in his typical style, "Oh, this will never last Karen. This was just luck that you got this auction. I bet you'll never get another one like this again since you weren't all that good anyway."

Once again, I remembered my dad being so critical due to his inability to succeed and my innate desire to succeed. He was unable to love himself enough to actually be proud of me. I just hugged him goodnight and said, "Dad, I love you. I only hope you can realize I am already successful, I know that I am doing what I love, and someday I will give you all the credit. I was able to get past your criticism and love myself enough to know that if one does not get past their hurt, one can never reach their potential. You see, Dad, I am what you wanted to be, and that is okay. I will continue to thank you and love you for all I am because of you. I will be successful, and hopefully some day you will be proud. But I am not going to spend one more day trying to make you proud of me." It was not until he laid on his deathbed that he was able to tell me that he was indeed proud of me.

Many of life's most meaningful rewards and blessings require us to successfully overcome some type of challenge, whether it is pain or fear. Making meaningful changes on a personal level requires willingness to make an honest evaluation of "self" and courage to try something new. When we come to a point where we are willing to say, "Hey, I have nothing to lose and only have room for improvement," we put ourselves in a vulnerable position for unprecedented blessings. However, it takes courage to move out of your comfort zone towards uncharted territory, even if that comfort is your own pain and struggle. The more willing you are to face your struggle, the more blessings you will enjoy. Learning to view challenges as adventures and struggles as excitement will change the way you experience your life. I encourage you to train yourself to look beyond the pain and struggle and see the rewards that courage brings. Focus on the blessing; it is yours for the taking.

After I had about fifty charity auctions under my belt that first year, I decided to keep going forward with my passion and forget about all the excuses that were allowing me to stay in my comfort zone. I needed to know if anyone was doing this full time, and

I wondered if an auctioneer could specialize in charity auctions without ever facilitating any other type of event.

There were auction companies who wrote books on how to put together benefit and charity auctions and how to run silent and live auctions, but I had never met anyone who claimed fundraising as their career choice. This was going to be my purpose, and whatever followed was fine with me as long as I knew I was making a difference. While I had already joined the National Association of Auctioneer (NAA) and the Minnesota State Auctioneer Association, I had no particular individual from whom I could learn. The only thing I could do was make mistakes, but regardless of the number of mistakes I made, I was driven to learn from them and keep moving forward.

## Your Fourth and Final Wing: Compassionate Skills

Now let's talk about your fourth and final butterfly wing: your compassionate skills. Skills are defined as the ability to do something with expertise. They are something that may have always come naturally to you, or more than likely, you may have had to work hard to gain these skills through education and experience. As you can begin to tell, your sweet spot will be found right in the middle of your compassionate hobby and your skillset.

Your skills are a major piece to the role you will play in your personal story and in the bigger story of the world in which we all play a role. Look at your skills in the same way a lumberjack looks at his ax. He constantly works to sharpen his ax and learn how to wield its power better with greater and greater efficiency. We should do the same with our skills. After all, it has more than likely taken a big piece of your life to build these skills, and you did this for a purpose whether you knew it or not.

When I first went to auction school, I had no idea I would eventually be serving with my auction skills for non-profit organizations around the world. Through it all, though, I remained open and receptive to how God wanted to use my newfound skill to the benefit of others and His glory. I encourage you to remain open as well. It makes a huge difference when we look and pay attention to how we are being guided because we all are.

Your skills are actually tools you will use to win hearts and truly give of yourself to the world. Go back to the words you wrote down during the discussion of your first butterfly wing, and think about all the ways in which your heart feels inspired. God truly does give us these skills and loves when we use them to freely give and speak into people's hearts. To give and give in abundance is the purpose for your skills. To determine how to use your skills: ask. Pray, and God will guide you. Write down the skills you have. Don't forget about all the skills you've had throughout your entire life, especially the skills you once had that have been forgotten or lost. Those skills can be resurrected. Sometimes our greatest skills get abandoned when they are put to shame by others or by our own self.

Maybe you had an absolute passion for playing guitar, but the first time you played for anyone, you were mocked and put the guitar away forever. What was meant for glory ended up being put to shame. You may have wanted to be a great basketball player but didn't even make the team your freshman year, so you decided to put that dream on the shelf for embarrassment's sake.

What was meant for glory ended up being put to shame. Good thing Michael Jordan didn't quit after he didn't make the cut his freshmen year. Recall the different ways you have been put to shame. There are reasons for this, you know. How were some of your early talents or skills put to shame? What are you going to do about it?

Recover these skills. Bring them back to life with a renewed enthusiasm, a resolute resolve, and a committed heart.

## Be a Finisher

When it comes to harnessing and forging truly valuable skillsets, we must learn to be a finisher. A finisher is a person who completes the job and sees the task through to the end. In order to truly sharpen your skills and serve others at a higher level, finishing what you start will be paramount. Don't let fear of failure get in your way. Refuse to let temporary setbacks frustrate you. Understand that building these skills takes time.

Your first step will be to totally commit to a plan of action that will allow you to build the necessary skillsets. I guarantee committing to this plan will be much harder than you think in the beginning. I tell you this not to discourage you, but rather to help prepare you for the road ahead.

It may help to think of it in relation to three runners all training to run a marathon. Now, before discussing their training methods, you must be aware of "the wall." The wall typically happens somewhere between mile eighteen and twenty. When a runner hits the wall, their body starts to shut down, they feel tremendous pain, and their number one thought is to quit. The only way to get through the wall is to keep running no matter what; that is the only solution.

Now the first marathon runner does not know the wall exists. He trains hard, but in the back of his mind he is really content with just running the race and doesn't really expect to finish. The second runner is absolutely committed to finishing the marathon and trains like it. She trains every single day, stays true to her diet no matter what, and makes sure she gets the recommended amounts of sleep every night. She has total belief she can finish the race and has every intention to finish. The problem is she has no knowledge of the wall. She doesn't know what happens when she will hit the wall, doesn't know everyone else who finishes the race will hit the wall, and does not understand what her body will feel like when this happens. The third marathon runner fully expects to finish, trains to finish, and has a full understanding of the wall, its effects on her body, and how to move beyond it to reach her goal.

On race day, the first runner makes it to mile twelve, gets tired, and quits because he didn't expect to finish in the first place. The second competitor is running strong until she hits the wall. Because she doesn't understand the wall exists, as soon as her body starts shutting down with pain shooting through her legs, she thinks something is wrong. She never anticipated this, and she quits because she thinks something bad is happening.

The third marathon runner, as expected, runs a strong race, hits the wall, and because of her understanding and anticipation, keeps moving forward. She feels the same pain with her body shutting down in the same manner the second runner felt, but she anticipated the wall coming. She finished because she knew what was ahead, was totally committed, and never lost sight of the finish line.

I tell you this story to illustrate my point. Building your skills will take time, you will have setbacks, and it will be totally, absolutely worth every single minute.

*What are some skills you have that others tend to notice and value?*

_____

_____

_____

*What are some unexpected or unseen ways you serve others?*

_____

_____

_____

*What skills do you have or could you develop that would allow you to serve others in a greater way?*

_____

_____

_____

If nothing changes, there would be
no butterflies.

                              - Author Unknown

# 9

## Necessary Endings

**MY AUCTION CAREER** continued to grow, and I strongly felt I had found a vehicle to fulfill and serve my purpose of making a difference in the lives of those less fortunate. My family, however, always came first.

I felt that as long as Matt and Sunny were still at home, I would fulfill my role as a mother and continue to be thankful that I was blessed with these two children. I recall many of my friends eagerly waiting for their kids to grow up. I, on the other hand, loved my role as mother and nurturer more than anything else.

When the kids were in their teens, they naturally became more independent and involved in all their activities. My husband eventually took a job offer on the east coast, which meant he commuted back and forth every other week.

While it was challenging, I managed to balance taking care of two teenagers while conducting auctions on the weekends. The emotional distance between my husband and I already felt like we were a thousand miles apart before he even left, and the actual physical distance only sped up the inevitable. Our nineteen-year marriage slowly started to crumble.

There were days when Matt and Sunny did all sorts of crazy things, and I wondered how I was ever going to get through those years. Even though I was married to a man that provided for us financially, in his physical absence, I was thrown into the day-to-day responsibilities of raising two teenagers on my own. As you can imagine, this required me to constantly put out fires and handle many different crises that happen in the life of a teenager.

I'll never forget the day I received a call from the high school telling me my son had been expelled for wearing the other football team's mascot uniform. What? Are you kidding me? Did he hurt someone? Did he hurt himself?

When I saw him, I simply hugged him and reminded him there may be rules we do not understand, but we still must obey. Embracing him, I reminded him that regardless of the circumstances, he must simply love, live, and learn. Through this escapade with my son, it was as if I was living my childhood over again when I was punished for really doing nothing wrong.

Of course, with a beautiful teenage daughter, I helped encourage and dry her tears through many breakups. There were concussions, broken bones, shattered spirits, and even my own denial at times. One day, as I was going through my fifteen-year-old baby girl's dance bag in order to wash her dance clothes, I found a full clear bottle of Pepsi. Shocked, I found myself in the moment wondering if there was a new kind of Pepsi that was clear, only to open the bottle and smell that it was pure Vodka.

When she returned home from school, I remarked, by holding up the bottle, "Sunny, we need to return this Pepsi as it has only water in it!"

She responded, "Okay, Mom. Stupid is not written across your forehead; I can explain." That was only one of many incidents, but I continued to be thankful that I was even blessed with children.

I felt so alone to deal with these problems of raising teens, and there were many times I felt completely inadequate to help them learn, cope, and keep moving forward. I remember envying my friends who had their husbands to help deal with the kids and their antics, but as always, I wouldn't allow myself to stay rooted in self-pity. Having my back against the wall and feeling totally alone left me with only one option: figure it out. Through hard work and grace, I kept moving forward for my children's sake while never forgetting about my other children in the *National Geographic* magazine.

After raising two teenagers and handling everything that accompanied that time, I knew at that point I was strong enough to handle anything on my own. I felt the strength to be able to deal with all the frustrations, drama, and misfortunes that life could throw at me. As I came to this realization, it signaled the end of my marriage. I moved on knowing I was free to live as I truly desired, and that I was capable of doing so. It was the end to one of the biggest chapters of my life. My children, Matthew and Sunny, were becoming my greatest teachers.

## Some Things Must Come to an End

We all have things in our life that we know must stop but have such a hard time actually putting an end to them. This is one of the biggest human dramas: we know what to do, we don't do it, and we don't know why we don't do it.

## Examples of this human drama abound.

We absolutely know if we burn more calories than we eat, we will lose weight. Yet there are books upon books written on the subject of losing weight. I know when I walk into a coffee shop that ordering water or an orange slushy is healthier for me, but what do I do? The same thing millions of other Americans do every single day; I order coffee. I know it isn't healthy for me, but I do it anyways.

The point is, we all know some things we can do today to improve our life. We know them, but we don't do them, at least not consistently. This applies no more fully than in the necessary endings we must have in our life.

When we truly experience personal growth or transformation, we shed things from our life, things that have been in our life for years and even decades. Some of these things we've carried with us our entire lives. These necessary endings are the people, events, or habits that we know we must get rid of, but we don't. We avoid it. We make up excuses and find other things, anything, to avoid it.

Have you ever noticed how great you feel when you follow through with what you know you ought to do? This is what happens when we are acting in alignment with our truest values and our most intense dreams. The fact is, endings are a natural part of a healthy life. This doesn't, however, stop all the hesitation and discomfort that arises when ending things we know must be ended.

## Butterfly Segway and Wrap-Up

Now you see how crucial it is to find your wings and how hard life is to make sense of when our wings are missing. It breaks my heart to see how many people have the spirit of a butterfly yet are still caterpillars. They have the spirit, the desire, and the potential to fly, but they must find their wings first.

I am breaking this book up into two distinct phases. You've read through the first phase where you know my story and everything I went through to find my wings. I hope in sharing my story, you found a piece of yourself in it along with the strength to move forward. I hope you are inspired to look through your past, shed what you don't want from it, and move forward into the future.

Now we venture into a little taste of what my life has been since I found my wings and took flight with God's help. I want to continue my story to inspire you to look forward to the goodness God has for you in this world and all the amazing things that happen when you find your wings.

This is the story about life, love, and crocodile teeth.

🦋

Happiness is like a butterfly; the more you chase it, the more it will elude you, but if you turn your attention to other things, it will come and sit softly on your shoulder.

— Thoreau

# 10

## Obrigado Deus!

**FAST FORWARD.** It is now 2007, I've been divorced for seven years, the kids have graduated from college, and I have again claimed my independent spirit. I embraced my career, was living my purpose, and could not be more fulfilled.

I tried to fill the void of my nineteen-year empty marriage with several relationships, some of which were very interesting to say the least. With each of my five ended relationships, I adopted one cat. At least the humane society loved me! Each of my five cats represented one man I was in a relationship with that didn't work. I needed to stop this nonsense. I simply did not have the time or energy to try to find love, especially after all these failed relation-ships. I couldn't afford another cat.

But through it all, something wonderful was happening inside me. As I was gradually accepting the person I had become, love was beginning to find me.

## Zau 37 @ g

In 2007, Sunny had just graduated from college, and my gift to her was an opportunity to go on a trip anywhere in the world. I was hoping she would choose Australia (which I let her know), but this was not about me, as she reminded me. She chose Brazil. Of course I had to share my opinion that Rio de Janeiro was the ultimate Den of Iniquity. All I could think about was drunken carnival people lusting after scantily clad Brazilian women, crime around every corner, and no sense of direction or purpose. You may have heard the statement warning you to be careful of your words, as you may have to eat them someday.

We were not in Brazil more than twenty-four hours when my purse was stolen. The very next day, Sunny ended up with Montezuma's Revenge from eating something we bought on the beach. To top it all off, we had several little street kids trying to pickpocket us. I couldn't resist reminding Sunny of my warnings about traveling to Brazil.

The next week we immersed ourselves in all of what Rio de Janeiro was truly about. We did the typical tours of the Christ Statue and Sugarloaf. We hiked through a tropical rainforest. One day, we decided to take a tour of one of the most dangerous and poor Favela's (slums) in the world. 225,000 poor and disadvantaged people live in the side of a mountain. The sights and sounds were forever imbedded in our minds. Poverty and crime was around every corner. Twelve-year-old boys were carrying guns. Trash heaped in piles as we continued to walk the many steep steps up to the top of the mountain. It seemed as though my *National Geographic* children were coming to life.

On one particularly hot day while walking along Copacabana

Beach, we noticed many street people selling their wares. One man in particular caught my attention, not for the way he looked, but for his energy. His energy was undeniable, and it drew me to him. He was selling his jewelry on the other side of the beach walkway. I insisted we go see what he was selling as this would give me the opportunity to check out why I was so drawn to him. Sunny was reluctant to say the least. She pointed out the obvious: he was a street person. It was true, as I looked closer; he was absolutely filthy.

In an attempt to see if he recognized my energy, I yelled and waved, "Hello, Hello!"

The second he looked at me, it immediately felt like a magnet.

I persisted and said, "Just for a minute, Sunny."

My daughter replied, "Mom, you do not need any jewelry nor do you need a man." She was right. After being married to her father for nineteen years and divorced by this time for nearly eight, I indeed was not looking for a man. I was independent and loving my freedom! I was in the middle of delving myself into my work along with all the other things I wanted to do now that my last child was all grown up, and I didn't have to ask for anyone's permission.

As we scurried across the road, trying to avoid all the cars and hundreds of people, my mind was racing. The man looked more African than Brazilian. He had long dreadlocks with several silver earrings intertwined between each dread. His earrings looked more like weapons than accessories. He definitely had not seen a shower or razor for weeks, but still I was drawn to his energy.

As we approached him, my daughter indicated that she had her reservations of this uniquely different man. To ease her mind, I promised her I wouldn't touch him.

Sunny and I moved closer and closer until I was within

talking-distance. I proceeded to ask about his jewelry when, right in the middle of our conversation and absolutely out of nowhere, he fell to his knees and exclaimed "Obrigado Deus!"

I knew enough Portuguese to know that he was saying, "Thank you, God."

My daughter immediately said, "Mom, of course he thanks God! You are beautiful, American, and his ticket!"

Right when she said that, I had a feeling he was my ticket, and I told this to Sunny. Even though I didn't know where this ticket would take me, I just knew that we met for some reason.

At that moment I wanted to ask him a million questions. Did he feel the same energy as I did? How did he get to Brazil? Did he actually live on the streets? Why was his jewelry different then all the other hippies selling their wares? Each piece of his jewelry was unique, appearing tribal in appearance. To me it looked as if the material he used came from the Amazon region of Brazil. He didn't have any rip-off jewelry or spin-off brand clothes like many of the others.

The conversation ended rather quickly after hello, as he only spoke Portuguese. However, when I asked him where he was from, he replied, "Angola, Africa." I am assuming he had this question asked of him before in a variety of languages.

As grace would have it, one of his Brazilian street friends knew a little English. This friend proceeded to explain that when we first waved to this man (I'll call him Mr. Dreadlocks for now), he didn't even think I was waving at him. He actually told his friends, "There is no way those girls are waving at me. I look like a monkey."

Was I attracted to him? No! Not like when you meet someone and thoughts of a relationship enter your mind. And I definitely wasn't in the habit of dating every homeless African/Brazilian jewelry maker I see on the streets of Rio de Janeiro. Thank God for that! I'd have to get a tiger instead of another cat to cover up for this one!

So, I decided in order for me to have any connection to Mr. Dreadlocks, I would buy a piece of his jewelry. I thought at least I would take a part of him home with me if I never saw him again. His energy would be in the jewelry. I bought some jewelry and told him I would see him tomorrow at 4:00 P.M. before we returned to the United States.

Sunny did not believe we would ever see him again, and who could blame her. She kept asking, "What are you thinking? You are leading him on!"

I told her we would see if the connection and energy was still there the next day or if it was indeed the two *cervezas* (beers) I had consumed earlier that day.

The next day, when I went to look for Mr. Dreadlocks, he was not there. My daughter said, "See, Mom. Look what I told you. Let's go. We need to catch the shuttle." At this point, I could still feel his energy, but I had to turn back around and face the fact that we needed to catch the shuttle.

We were no more than five steps in our turnaround when I heard a voice, "Linda, Linda, ola Linda!" (Which means lady in Portuguese).

He did remember to come back. Our time was limited, but I decided to move out of my comfort zone and dare to ask if he had an e-mail address. He responded by immediately running off, leaving his backpack and his display of jewelry right where we stood. My daughter was the rational one this time and kept reminding me we had a shuttle to catch.

I insisted that we wait because I knew he would be back, which held true. He returned a couple minutes later dripping in sweat with a pencil that had broken lead. Peeling the pencil wood back to expose the remaining lead, he attempted to jot down his e-mail. However, he was shaking so profusely he was unable to finish his entire e-mail. It ended at "Zau 37 @ g." I then wrote mine down for him as Sunny stood in disbelief that I would ever again communicate with this man. This was just crazy.

And, let me tell you, it was about to get even crazier. When you are flying with your newly found and hard-earned wings, you are going to have moments in your life where you know the only explanation of the goodness you receive is pure grace. This was one of those moments.

Upon my arrival back in the U.S., I needed to check all of my e-mails as back then I did not have a Blackberry and only used an Internet café a couple times during our trip. I scrolled through the hundreds of e-mails, and low and behold, there was one from zau37@gmail.com.

I thought to myself, "You've got to be kidding? Is this really the man I left back in Brazil 27 hours ago?" I was shaking as I opened the e-mail but soon realized it was all in Portuguese. I wanted so desperately to know what he was writing to me.

I immediately called Sunny and asked her how to translate Portuguese to English. Everyone in my immediate circle knows I am totally computer illiterate. Reluctantly, she instructed me how to use dictionary.com to translate, and it didn't sound too difficult. I was on a mission.

When the translation came across my screen, I was over-whelmed as this man could finally communicate his feelings. His words were kind and caring. He wanted to make sure I was home safely and that all was well in my world. He went on to simply thank me for buying a piece of his jewelry so he could finally enjoy a good meal. He made no mention of any feelings he might have for me. He ended his e-mail with…Obrigado Deus…Thank you God.

I was tired from my trip, and I needed to recover along with catching up on all the tasks that accumulate when a business owner goes on vacation. A couple days passed, but I continued to feel an undeniable energy from this man unlike anything I had ever experienced in my life. I couldn't even get myself to take off the necklace I bought from him. I decided to reply to the e-mail he sent two days ago.

I kept the email short and sweet. I simply asked some questions that were grilling my own mind:

*Is selling jewelry your living?*

*Do you live on the street?*

*How did you get to Brazil?*

*Where did you get the material for your jewelry?*

And finally…

*Did you kill the crocodile for his teeth in your ears?*

It seemed like an eternity to get a response from him. Days went by slowly, and I resigned myself to thinking that I had a once-in-a-lifetime meeting, and that was all it was. It was over now I thought.

One week later, I received a response!

He started by apologizing that it took him so long to respond, but he needed to sell enough jewelry in order to eat and then to buy Internet time to e-mail me. His ability to be so open and honest left me thinking this was the richest man I have ever met in my life. He went on to share that he needed to go back to the Amazon for more material from the Indians. He explained that he learned the jewelry trade from the Indians with whom he had lived for many years. He then informed me he would not have access to a computer for a very long time.

When I read that, I immediately felt a wild dare! Why not meet him and travel up the Amazon River together? Why not travel from my comfortable home in Minnesota down to the outskirts of the Amazon to meet a man who roamed the jungle. A man that I have met for a grand total of twenty minutes and a man with whom I've only exchanged a few emails.

Makes perfect sense…right?

How could I be getting these ideas?

At this time, I was just experimenting with a documentary film. What a perfect excuse to see him again! I had always yearned to be behind the camera and study people in developing countries anyway. Here was my opportunity to see my *National Geographic* children in real life, the children I had dreamed about helping since childhood! This was my chance! Was it? Or was I crazy?

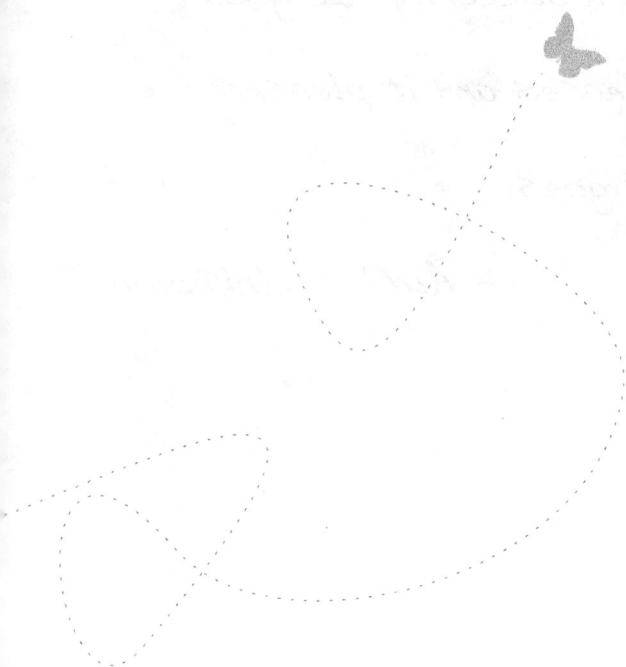

Love is like a butterfly: It goes
where it pleases and it pleases
wherever it goes.

- Author Unknown

# 11

## Crocodile Teeth and Malaria

**OUT OF THE COMFORT** zone I wanted to go once again! Thoughts raced through my head as I e-mailed him back with this crazy idea of mine.

He responded in a tone that made it sound like it was no big deal. He welcomed the thought and told me when and where I could meet him.

How many blonde haired former Mrs. Minnesota's had this guy hooked up with?! What a crazy thought. Sometimes you just have to go with it, and that is what I was doing. I immediately looked at my auction schedule, and I had ten days before my next auction – perfect! I booked my tickets and planned for my trip into the unknown.

I knew I was headed into the jungle and needed to be protected from all sorts of things, especially in that region of the world where sicknesses such as malaria are prevalent. I immediately made an appointment with my doctor to get all the necessary shots and medications: yellow fever, hepatitis A & B, and malaria pills. I was leaving in three days, and the directions for the malaria pills stated it took seven days for the medication to take effect. I rationalized to myself, thinking four days couldn't make that much of a difference, and I took off!

I sent him my itinerary, and we made plans to meet. We would then head on our way without any help or assistance of any kind from anyone, especially not from Dictionary.com. It is interesting how we used technology to communicate. Usually when you hear of couples meeting and initially communicating over the Internet, it is related to Match.com and people living just across town. For me, it was Dicitonary.com to translate languages and communicate with a man I met across the globe. I never gave it a second thought as to how we would communicate on our trip up the Amazon to visit the Indians. Who needs to worry about details?

The day before I left, I told my mother I needed a ride to the airport. When she asked me why I was leaving again when I had just returned from Brazil two weeks earlier, I simply responded, "I'm going on an adventure."

She didn't understand what kind of adventure would take me back to Brazil with cameras in hand. My mother was well aware of my interest in photography and indigenous people in distant lands, but she still did not understand and I didn't want to tell her everything.

So my journey began.

After twenty-nine hours of going from one flight to another, I arrived at the airport where we had agreed to meet. Everything was perfect except for the fact that he was not there!

Perhaps he was running late. So I did another thing totally out of my comfort zone: I waited. I sat, alone with my thoughts.

"What if he changed his mind?"

"Was I to turn back and fly home?"

"Are you kidding me?"

I had come a long way, and I was going on this adventure with or without Mr. Dreadlocks. Now granted, most people who plan a trip to the Amazon River in Brazil plan it for months in advance. It took me only a few days to say yes and get to Brazil!

I decided I would allow this man's energy to bring me to him. Is this crazy?! Of course it was crazy! Did I realize at the time how large the city of Santarem, Brazil was? Was I fearless or stupid?

I first went to the Currency Exchange and converted my dollars to reais. Then I set out to find an English-speaking taxi driver. Upon entering a taxi, I handed a piece of paper to the driver with the approximate location Zau, (Mr. Dreadlocks real name), told me we would be catching a boat to begin our journey. Did the taxi know where this was, or was he going to take me somewhere else? Was I scared? Perhaps a little, but I was destined to find this man. After one hour, the taxi pulled over and said, *"Aqui, Aqui custa …60 reais."* How much was that in dollars? I never had time to figure out the exchange rate. He could have been asking me for 100 dollars. I gave him what he asked, grabbed my backpack, and flew out the door.

My destination appeared to resemble what Zau was talking about: thousands of people near the river. This was the Amazon River? It was huge, dirty, and the boats were scary! There were hundreds of people everywhere. Was Zau here? Would I be able to find him?

I was exhausted from my trip and needed to somehow communicate with Zau. At that moment, I saw an Internet café. Ah ha! Maybe if I e-mailed him, he would know I was here and could explain why he forgot to pick me up at the airport!

I sat down at the filthiest computer I had ever touched. The keyboard was covered with so much dirt that I had to tap the keys forcefully in order for them to type anything.

I proceeded with a very short e-mail:

"It's me. I got on my connecting flight to Santarem and you were not there as you said you would be. You must have a good reason. I hope you are OK. I hope you arrived safely. I have taken a taxi, and I am at an Internet café wondering where you are. I will now go and try to find you among the street people selling jewelry; perhaps they will know you. I will check back in three hours to see if you have responded to this e-mail. If not, I believe everything happens for a reason, and I only wish you well. I am a big girl and will be fine. I will enjoy this short adventure and then decide what I will do if I do not hear back from you.

*Obrigado Deus.*

Off I went on my search for Zau, the man with the crocodile teeth earrings. I arrived in the area he spoke about where hippies sold their crafts to tourists. I did not waste any time. I came across the first hippie I saw and asked, *"Desculpa, voce falo englesh?"* (Do you speak English?)

I only got *"Desculpa, eu nao falo englesh,"* which meant "Sorry, I do not speak English!" I was not going to give up. I did have a picture of him that he sent me in an e-mail, so I pulled that out and began by saying his name: Zau. I walked up and down the street saying, " Zau, Zau." Finally, a very frail looking Indian came up and spoke with broken English. He said, *"Zau aeuroporto,"* as he glanced up in the sky.

I pleaded with him, "Did Zau go to the airport?" He replied, *"Linda, Americana"* (American lady).

Yes! This had to mean Zau's friend was telling me he went to the airport to find me. I did not know what to do next. Should I go back to the Internet café to see if I received a response? No, it was too soon.

I did know I needed a hotel regardless of whether or not I connected with Zau. I went in and out of every hotel to find a rate within my budget, as hotels are expensive in Brazil. After walking over a mile, I found one, checked in, and decided to take a shower. For $150 U.S. dollars, there was only cold water, but I didn't mind the cool shower. It was over 100 degrees outside, and the hotel's air conditioning barely worked.

Feeling a bit more refreshed, I left my backpack at the hotel and headed out again on my search with just a little pouch of money. I checked my e-mail and found nothing. Hours passed, and while I was disheartened at not finding Zau, I decided to make the most of the journey. I needed something to eat and found a great little place on a corner where I could sit and people watch. Ok, now what?

I took in more sights, and I was actually enjoying myself. The sights and sounds were all so new to me. I decided to go down and see where the boats load people and take them on their journey up the Amazon, which eventually led me to a very busy street. As the light turned green, I walked with all the other hundreds of people across the street. Out of nowhere, there was Zau standing on the opposite corner.

I thought I was hallucinating. No way could this actually be him. Had I gone crazy? I shouted with my hand up high, "Hello, hello Zau! It is me, it is me!"

Then he too mimicked the same phrase "Karen, Karen! Hello! Oi Oi". I could not believe this. There was no way other than Divine intervention that we would meet on this busy street corner. I embraced him and kept asking him why he wasn't at the airport as we had planned. He pulled out the itinerary and showed me the "P.M." He then repeated, "A.M. A.M. Airport!" I finally figured out he went to the airport twelve hours before I arrived. He mixed up the A.M. and P.M.!

He continued speaking in Portuguese, pointing to his backpack and then to my back. He wondered where my backpack was. I pointed to the hotel and told him it was there. How were we going to communicate? We needed to figure this out.

After a couple of beers and trying to get through our language barrier, we decided not to waste any more time, so we went back to the hotel, grabbed my backpack, paid for a night I never used, and started our journey. We soon connected with what appeared to be some of his friends. I was just going along on the ride. Little did I know there were no bathrooms on the boat. I saw many boats with a lot of people, and I knew they had to have bathrooms. Why did I not suggest we go up the Amazon on one of those Hilton on water wheels? It had not even been an hour after checking out of the hotel and drinking a couple of *cervezas*, and they were going right through me!

I motioned to Zau that I needed to use the bathroom, but the problem was, there was no bathroom. He instructed me to lift up my skirt and pee over the side of the boat.

Are you kidding me?! I get disgusted at public restrooms, let alone peeing over the side of a boat! But, I had no choice, so I got the job done and peed over the side of a nasty boat right in the middle of the Amazon River.

The next few hours went by like minutes. I completely let go of any thoughts of work back home. I forgot about all the e-mails I needed to answer and the questions people had about why I was returning to Brazil so soon to head up the Amazon with a man I barely knew. For whatever reason, though, I can honestly say I felt safer in that boat with Zau than I ever had before in my life. Being in his presence was like a gift from God.

Eventually, darkness fell. Would we stop? Were we going to pitch a tent? Where was I going to sleep? When I tried to ask this simple question, I was met with the answer in a gesture of a backpack that would be used for a pillow and a tarp that would be my blanket. Was it going to get cold? Was the boat going to tip? I had more questions than a kindergartner on their first day of school.

That night, the rains came. It didn't seem to bother anyone else, so why should it bother me? I had to become a tomboy again. There was no crying or complaining. I was using the skills my father taught me to survive the river.

I must have dozed off for several hours, as when I awoke, we had arrived at a village along the banks. We were welcomed by Indians who did not resemble what I thought Indians would look like. In fact, one of the men who helped us with the boat was wearing an Adidas shirt. Another Indian man wore a baseball cap with "NY" embroidered on the front.

I soon found out that this is how they traded merchandise. Zau needed their natural products, and in return, he gave them what they wanted and needed most: clothes. They had no use for money.

I soon found out we had to continue our trip as they did not have the product or materials Zau needed to make his jewelry. So we continued on our journey. At one point, I held up two fingers and said, "How long up the river: two days, three days? Zau responded with nine fingers. I just about fell off the boat! I couldn't be up the river for nine days. I barely survived one day! No bathrooms, no showers, and now I officially started to panic. I was crazy. This was a very insane, crazy idea, and it was catching up to me all at once. What was I thinking? Oh my…literally?

I told Zau I wanted to go back. I kept pointing in the direction from where we came. It did not seem to affect him, so we continued our journey. The next day, which now seemed like a week, we arrived at a more remote area. We left the boat and walked for what seemed to be hours.

The long walk seemed worth the work when I saw the Indians. I thought my blonde hair would take them aback, but it did not seem to faze them. I wanted so much to be able to speak their language. I felt like I was six again when I did not talk much or show any emotion. I had grown so far past that to find my butterfly wings and become a fundraising auctioneer where all I knew how to do was talk. Now, I felt alone with my language barrier.

That night we camped in the village. This was the first time I slept in a hammock that was closed so tight I could hardly move.

I was later told through pictures that if you do not wrap yourself tightly, snakes will eventually become your bed partner.

During the rainy, wet morning, I learned all about the Acai berry and the crocodile as Zau wheeled and dealed over the product he needed.

At one point, Zau noticed that I appeared to be feeling scared and alone. He came over to me, took his dreadlocks, and put them over my shoulder as if it was his arm. I tried not to cry. With our language barrier, all he could do was comfort me with a beautiful silence, as if everything would be all right.

Two days later, I began feeling shaky and sweaty. Then dizziness set in, but still I tried to ignore it. Eventually, I became so sick I could not even think straight. I tried to get up but was overwhelmed with dizziness.

Could I have malaria? There was no doubt in my mind or Zau's that I was sick. I needed help, and I needed help fast. Whatever this sickness was, it came on quickly. I thought malaria took days to show signs. This could not be happening. I found out later that Zau had contracted malaria over five times in his life. I do not know what transpired the rest of that day. All I remember is the Indian ladies taking care of me through bouts of diarrhea and throwing up. It was the most God-awful feeling in the world.

⚘

*If you have the freedom to fly*

*why not take the scenic route.*

*— Claire Williams*

# 12

## Saved by Dreadlocks

**NOT EVEN WHEN** I was paralyzed for an entire school year had I felt this sick before. I really do not recall much from this episode in the jungle, but I think I remember the big moments.

I was uncontrollably shaking. I could not tell if it was hours that were passing or days, but I didn't even care. All I knew is it felt like years to me and that I was close to going home to see Jesus. I knew I had to hold on and make it through. But malaria? I didn't know much about this except that people die. One thing I was certain of though was the absolute fact I was not ready to die. Thoughts kept racing through my mind. No one knows that I am sick. What will happen if I never come home? When and how will they find out I died?

By this point in my life, I was a big girl capable of taking care of myself, and my kids were young adults carrying on their own lives. My 82-year-old mother was always worried about what I was getting into, but she would never guess that I spent a few days inadvertently having the eggs of a mosquito planted in me and almost dying right in the heart of the Amazon jungle! As I laid there, I desperately tried to stay positive while holding on to the truth that my life was indeed in God's hands.

Eventually, my fever took its toll, and the next thing I knew, I was swallowing something that tasted like alcohol. I at least thought I could get drunk enough to forget what happened and escape the misery of my pain. My head was pounding. My body was shaking.

Without knowing how much time had elapsed, I soon started to feel an undeniable belief that I was going to make it through this ordeal. My time was not up. God wasn't done with me yet! When I finally began feeling somewhat normal, I only then realized that this kind man I met three weeks ago in Rio de Janeiro saved my life. Zau actually cared enough to abandon his path to help me get back on mine. And did he ever!

We both knew our journey in the jungle had to stop here. There was no question he had to get me back and send me home. My journey was coming to an unexpected and immediate halt, just as quickly as it had begun.

It seemed like weeks, but we finally made it back to where our journey started. I was so weak. I needed a bed. I needed food. I needed a shower. I knew I needed to get checked into a hotel, and I needed to do it quickly. The nasty Brazilian shower was the most comforting and welcome site I had ever seen!

But what was I going to do with my rescuer, with Zau? Was I just going to leave this man to sleep on the street after he saved my life? I couldn't think of it. Still unable to speak the same language,

I motioned for him to take a shower and get himself cleaned up.

Up until this point, I never had those feelings you get when you think you are falling in love: your heart goes pitter-patter and you get butterflies in your stomach.

Now, when I looked at this man, I was overwhelmed with gratitude that he knew what to do to save my life. How did he know what to do? How did he do it? Where did he get the supplies? I had no idea. I didn't care. Just like I didn't care about his past, his shortcomings, or his dreadlocks. I began to see his heart, and the more his heart was revealed to me, the more I felt mine coming to the surface.

He proceeded to get into the shower. At that point, something came over me in my weak state, and I began to weep. Since crying was not part of my childhood, it was such a warm and foreign feeling. I couldn't describe it. As I embraced these feelings and let them pour over me, I realized the tears were those of joy and a thankful heart!

The man in the shower saved my life. I had a problem, though. This man had been in the shower for over forty minutes by this point. I couldn't help but think about what he was doing and worrying about why he had been in there so long. The thought never even dawned on me that this might be the very first shower of his life.

When he came out, it was as if he was a changed man. And why wouldn't he be? It was his first shower!

Then began the first date awkwardness with a jumble of feelings: the feelings of being up the Amazon River with a complete and total stranger you found on the streets, getting malaria, and being miraculously saved by a street hippie who just took a forty minute shower in your Brazilian hotel room. Okay, maybe this wasn't a first date, at least not a normal first date. All I knew is we were now in a hotel room, I was tired, he was tired, and there was only one bed. What's a girl to do? What was going to happen?

I knew I was too weak and still so sick that I had no thoughts of anything wild and romantic happening in that bed unless it was literally in my dreams. I was tired and so was he. Through more spontaneous sign language, I motioned for him to lay down on the bed and sleep next to me. Thoughts continued to run through my mind for a little bit before I fell asleep. Here I am in Brazil, just returning from the jungle, almost dying, laying in bed with a total stranger... a man for that matter. But this was a different kind of man. This man saved my life.

We eventually fell asleep. When I woke up, I went straight to the bathroom. Even though I was comparatively feeling much better, my internal plumbing now mirrored the pipes in this hotel; they weren't exactly working properly. As I was stumbling to the bathroom, I stumbled faster right into the bathroom door because Zau was now lying on the floor. What in God's name was he doing on the floor? Well, it turns out that Zau had never slept in a bed before. It was too uncomfortable for him, so he slept on the hard surface to which he was accustomed.

Everything about this man was making my heart grow and grow. Regardless of how sick I was and regardless of how much I resisted these new feelings, I couldn't deny them. Was I falling in love with this man? Was I actually falling in love with this street man with crocodile teeth in his ears? Is this what it felt like to fall in love? Was I ready for this? I was doing just fine on my own until the whole jungle experience. Should I tell him or show him in any way that I have feelings? My mind was racing!

I decided to just say, *"Obrigado"* over and over and over again, which means "Thank You!"

Zau repeatedly responded with *"Nada,"* which means, "No problem, you're welcome."

How sweet.

Now what?

Talk about long distance. We didn't even speak the same language yet; let alone being on separate sides of the planet.

Was I crazy, in love, or both?

I was forty-nine-years-old at this time and had never experienced feelings like this before. This had to be love. I felt like my feelings for this man and what he did for me made me more certain than ever that there is a God; He is love, and He loves us all!

With a grateful heart and awakened feelings of love, I was finally able to make the flight reservations to return home. When we said goodbye, I hugged Zau and never wanted to let him go. I wanted to pack him in my bag and take him home with me.

## Back to Life...and Minnesota

I eventually made it home to Minnesota and immediately checked myself into the travel clinic. They immediately began running tests on me. It took three back to back days in the hospital, three days of front and back needle pricks and blood slides from my fingers, three days to medically prove what I already knew and experienced: that I survived malaria. After all was said and done, the doctors actually speculated that I perhaps contracted malaria when I was in Brazil earlier with my daughter. We hiked in the rain forest, and at that time, there was a warning of a malaria outbreak. It usually takes two to three weeks to begin feeling the symptoms of malaria.

As I regained my strength, I could not get this man out of my mind. I sent him several e-mails thanking him. He replied in Portuguese, which my computer translated, and we continued to communicate. I eventually gathered up the nerve to tell him I had feelings for him and that I truly believed we would be together someday. Was I crazy or still delirious? I think both.

I had to go back to work. The first fundraising auction I did after my trip was horrible. I raised more money than the company anticipated, but in the middle of the auction, one of the bidders stopped bidding. Without thinking, I called out, "You wuss!"

What was I thinking? I had been given a new standard of giving, and the old standard had to go. Zau displayed and acted out generosity and compassion in ways I had never seen before. So when I returned to America and the gentleman in my audience would not continue bidding to full value on a trip to Hawaii, I would not stand for it. It didn't fit the new standard of giving Zau gave me.

I am not making excuses for insulting a donor in the audience during the middle of an auction. This was just the first time this new level of giving was emerging from me, and I didn't quite know how to handle it. I had a new standard, and I was beginning to carry this new standard to all of my events. I just needed to learn to express this new value in a way that would work with people and inspire them to give more, do more, and be more!

Despite my packed auction schedule, I felt compelled to return to Brazil and see Zau again. Not more than three weeks had passed since our adventure on the Amazon, but I more than missed him. I found myself longing to be with him again.

I looked at my calendar, and I had six days in between auctions.

Did I dare go back to Brazil and turn around in five days?

Why not?

I will do this.

I need to do this.

I must see this man again.

Over the next twelve months, I made six trips to Brazil and never looked back. It has been the greatest love story of my life. This kind of love makes you realize how good God is and how magical life can become when we find our wings and fly together.

This beautiful love story took an incredible amount of work. Homeland Security required me to place Zau in a rental in Brazil for one year to prove that he was not a street person. They refuse to interview anyone without a permanent address. The Visa process itself was not an easy task, either.

There are thousands of people per day at each U.S. Embassy in Brazil who apply for American Visas, and we were standing in an unimaginably long line. Of course, we were last in line because his name starts with a "Z." We arrived three hours before the embassy doors opened, and it took eight hours for the line to move around the building to the front. Needless to say, we were waiting there all day.

Out of all the US Consulates, my attention immediately turned to the only African American Consulate in the entire building. Something in me just knew he was the one with whom we needed to speak. He was the one who could get Zau into the US. All I could do was pray, and that is all I did while we were waiting. If we could somehow get to that man, I thought, we will make it.

The more and more people we saw turned away and denied the opportunity to enter the U.S., the more and more I prayed we would land on him. As yet another person was stamped "denied" and walked by us in disappointment, I literally extended my hand out in prayer with intense desire for God to lead us to that particular Consulate so Zau could make it to the U.S. My feelings for Zau were indescribable, as was our longing for him to join me in the United States. It was something we desperately desired, yet over which we had so little control.

Finally, *finally* we heard, "Francelino Zau, number 1,292." To my surprise, great joy, and complete relief, it was our man! Zau walked right up to his window. I will never forget the nervousness, anticipation, and frustration that I had all at the same time as Zau and the man for whom I had been praying carefully completed a mountain of paperwork. It seemed like Zau was standing there forever, and the gravity of the moment was filling my heart and the room, as I could do nothing but pray and wait.

I will never forget when he finally received his stamp: ACCEPTED! He was far away from me, but I could see him turn, look at me, and say, *"Obrigado Deus!"* Thank you, God!" In that moment, I knew that he was going to make it. My prayers had been answered, and we were over that hurdle! Like almost everything else in our relationship, I believe divine intervention is the only reason Zau's Visa was approved.

## Coming To America

After we had accomplished the daunting task of getting Zau's Visa miraculously approved, I needed to figure out how I was going to get him to the US. I spent days putting together a travel itinerary where I could meet him and personally make the trip over the border into the United States hand-in-hand with him. I found a way and booked his flight from Brazil to Peru to Costa Rica and we made plans to meet there.

I flew to Costa Rica, informing him (via Dictionary.com) that we would meet in Tamarindo, Costa Rica at a quaint little bar when his bus from San Jose arrived the evening of July 27th, 2008, but he didn't show. I didn't know what to think? I had now traveled to Brazil over six times, went through the rigorous Homeland Security Visa applications, rented Zau an apartment in Brazil for a year and had made all the necessary travel arrangements, but now he was missing!

As I waited impatiently, I asked the Spanish-speaking driver of the 8 P.M. bus if he remembered seeing a passenger with dreadlocks that spoke Spanish with a Cuban accent. He said, "No lady; no guy like that on my bus." I asked him what time the next bus arrived, and he told me around 11 A.M. the next day.

I then proceeded to the liquor store to buy myself a bottle of wine, returned to my hotel, looked in the mirror, and said, "Karen, are you crazy?!"

After feeling my wine and falling asleep, I heard a knock on my door at 2 A.M! The messenger exclaimed in broken English, "He is here! He is at the bar. He asked if there was an American woman staying here." Since Tamarindo is a small town, everyone knows what everyone else is doing, so they came to tell me that the man who saved my life was finally here!

⚶

Enjoy what God sends into your
life, the sunshine and the rain.
For His plan for you is that you
prosper and grow into the beautiful
creature he designed you to be.
For your time will come also to
soar like a Butterfly.

- Author Unknown

# 13

## My Butterfly

**I KNEW I WAS** in love with Zau, and now I could finally take him home! He was approved to stay in the U.S. for three months, during which time he would not only learn about a new culture, but also an entirely new way of living. What would he think of America and my way of life? It was up to me to use my butterfly wings, to carry my candle, and light the path for him with compassion and love.

Try to imagine growing up and living on the streets where the closest thing you ever had to a home was the shack you lived in during your days in Africa. You've lived your entire life making handicrafts and selling them for a piece of chicken. You've earned a living by rowing a boat deep into the Amazon jungle to barter for bare essentials that you will use to make jewelry to then sell on the same street upon which you sleep. This had been Zau's life, and now he was ushering in a new one, just as I was.

You see, we judge so easily and quickly based on appearance. The external transformation Zau went through, from living out of a backpack on the Brazilian streets to living in a beautiful home in Minnesota was obvious to anyone watching. Perhaps not as noticeable was the dramatic change my internal life was going through almost at the same time. On the outside looking in, I had it all: the career, the home, the car, the grown children, and many things. However, I had never felt unconditional love and acceptance like this before. While I was dramatically transforming from the inside-out, Zau was transforming from the outside-in. It was so beautiful that we were doing it together.

I can honestly say that Zau still, to this very day, has the exact same heart he had when I first saw him on that street corner. His surroundings have dramatically changed, but his compassionate heart is the same.

## First Time Home

When Zau walked into my house for the first time, he just stared. He didn't know what to say, I didn't know what to say, and even if we had words for the moment, we didn't communicate in the same language yet. He had never known the comfort of a home in the same way that I never knew the comfort of being truly and unconditionally loved.

At first, he wasn't comfortable sleeping on a bed, so he continued to sleep on the floor for a while. Then we had to introduce him to family. He had to go through all these "firsts." Imagine learning to live your life over again, experiencing your first meal in an actual home or preparing food in a kitchen as opposed to over a fire pit. All these first experiences were amazing to him and I was so grateful that I got to share them with him.

Nearly everything we take for granted each day, Zau was experiencing for the first time. And he was so grateful for being able to use these every day, ordinary conveniences we have come to expect. Even though all of this was new for him, his heart was the same as it was when he did not have these amenities. None of this made him happier, but it did profoundly change the way in which he lived. I felt a complete sense of peace and tranquility with Zau as he adapted into my lifestyle.

## American Women

After Zau settled into his new home, I had to teach him how to treat an American woman according to our culture, not the culture that he grew up with on the streets. They were two totally different worlds. I felt the frustration of trying to teach a different culture to a different person. Our courtship was hilarious because I had to lead the way on everything and teach him as I went along. Ladies, can you imagine teaching your husband how to date while you are dating him? Zau was so adorable through all the new lessons, though. He just kept stealing my heart more and more each day and with every date.

As I watched how fast he learned and adapted, I admired his humility.

It was a learning process for him and a renewal of my inner butterfly.

## Seven Pieces of Candy or Seven Bags of Candy?

Soon, it was Halloween. Zau didn't quite understand this strange American holiday where you dress up like the living dead, knock on strangers' doors, and receive a bunch of candy.

I tried explaining to him in the middle of Walgreens that we needed to get candy so we could hand it out to all the trick-or-treaters that would be coming. He was baffled. Of course, what would you think if you heard the word "trick-or-treaters" for the first time?

When he saw all the candy I was buying, all he said was, "Big boom-boom, you big boom-boom," while he pointed at my butt. He thought I was going to eat all the candy. I explained further that we would give this all away to the kids who came to our door. When I say explain, you have to remember I was speaking to him in English so he could learn, but he couldn't understand most of what I was saying to him. I demonstrated ringing the doorbell and saying, "Ding-dong," and then showed him how to give the candy away to the kids. I forgot to tell him there were going to be many kids, not just a one-time ding-dong at the door.

When we finally got back home, I explained to Zau that he needed to give the candy to the kids as they knocked on the door while I went downstairs to get ready for the Halloween party to which we had been invited. When I came back upstairs, excited to take a picture of him handing out candy on his first Halloween, all the candy was gone!

I asked him what happened to the candy, and he informed me he gave all the candy bags to the first kid who came to the door, and now there were none left! I laughed so hard, I cried. I can't count how many times these types of events happened.

Think about Thanksgiving, Christmas, and Easter. The fat bearded guy who comes down your chimney, the over-sized bunny who hides eggs for kids to find, these traditions were all new to my dearest Zau and so confusing. It was so cute and heartwarming to see how humble he was and how honestly he would ask the cutest little questions.

I, and everyone who met Zau, was taken aback and amazed by him.

## Tuxedos and Croc Teeth

I was so excited to further expose him to my world, especially a very important part of my world: my auctions! I remember the first auction I took him to: it was a fundraiser for the Children's Cancer Research. It was a ballroom auction, and Zau needed to wear a tux. He didn't even know what a tux was!

This, of course, would be the first time he ever wore a tux, and just getting it properly fitted was an experience. Zau couldn't believe they were marking white soap all over the tux! Why would we do such a thing? Just try to picture this from his point of view: we went to a store that basically sold the same kind of clothes rack after rack, they marked up his new clothes with white soap, we gave the store money to buy the clothes, and then we left the store with nothing! He was confused to say the least, and who could blame him!

After finding the appropriate attire, I was ready to take Zau to the big event. The auction was filled with highly educated, affluent achievers, and I was so proud to bring Zau with me. We were walking ten feet off the ground. I felt a passionate intensity just being around him. I was totally in love, couldn't control it, and didn't want to control it.

As I introduced Zau to all my friends at the gala event, some were in disbelief, some didn't know what to think, and absolutely everyone was shocked by this man I had with me. Zau left them awestruck with his new tuxedo, crocodile teeth in his ears, and the fact that he couldn't even speak English. However, I had learned long ago that to lead a truly inspired life, I had to free myself from other's expectations and judgments. I had fought hard to earn my butterfly wings, and Zau was lighting a path to my heart just as much as I was carrying the candle for him on his new American adventure.

It was so amazing to see him watch the fundraising videos of the kids we were helping that night at the auction. He started to understand why I was so passionate about what I was doing. He saw the children hooked up to the machines with no hair, and compassion welled in his heart. I could feel it.

The next event we went to was "Give Us Wings" from Africa. Zau was able to see the villages, much like the ones he grew up in, and the ways we were helping others. He saw the drinking wells we were funding in Uganda. While he didn't fully understand all that was happening, he certainly understood that whatever it was, was powerful. He understood goodness, and he understood doing good. He had an inner butterfly unlike anything I had ever experienced, and he understood what it meant to have compassion: first, last, and always.

I was overjoyed and so grateful. Zau's presence gave me a heightened sense of awareness, and I started to see my level of performance heighten as well. My skills were improving because of the motivation and inspiration Zau's love brought into my life. For me, this meant I had more fun raising money for causes I believed in, which translated into more money for my clients' charities. The compassionate skills of my fourth butterfly wing were developing even further as I experienced Zau's love for me and my love for him. Love never fails. Love never dies. Love always wins.

> If I speak in the tongues of men or of angels, but do not have love, I am only a resounding gong or a clanging cymbal. If I have the gift of prophecy and can fathom all mysteries and all knowledge, and if I have a faith that can move mountains, but do not have love, I am nothing. If I give all I possess to the poor and give over my body to hardship that I may boast, but do not have love, I gain nothing. Love is patient, love is kind. It does not envy, it does not boast, it is not proud. It does not dishonor others, it is not self-seeking, it is not easily angered, it keeps no record of wrongs. Love does not delight in evil but rejoices with the truth. It always protects, always trusts, always hopes, always perseveres. Love never fails. But where there are prophecies, they will cease; where there are tongues, they will be stilled; where there is knowledge, it will pass away. For we know in part and we prophesy in part, but when completeness comes, what is in part disappears.
>
> 1 Corinthians 13: 1-10 (NIV)

God sent Zau to complete and bring full circle all I had experienced in my life up to this point. The only thing that can complete me more than Zau is God himself. I had Zau, my faith in my God, and my butterfly wings, and nothing could stop me. I now understood that part of the joy that fills my heart is the love Zau shows me and the other part is the love God showed me. This is why Zau is still always with me at every event I facilitate. He makes me complete.

## Love and Be Loved

*"To love and to be loved is to feel the sun from both sides."*

*David Viscott*

I had to learn how to love and let someone love me back. Zau had to learn how to live and live in one of the craziest, busiest cultures in the world - America.

Even though we were not able to actually communicate with words for almost a year, we were able to communicate and share with each other through our hearts, our eyes, and our presence together. This was the most memorable part of our courtship. The only words we knew well enough in each other's language were "love" and "thank you, God."

In 2009, Zau and I became man and wife. While our spoken language barrier has dissolved since our miraculous first meeting, we still know well the words we relied upon for so long, and we remain grateful for the love and hand of God that brought us together.

Love is like a butterfly, it settles

upon you when you least expect it.

— Author Unknown

# Conclusion and Thank You

I want to thank you for allowing me to share my story with you. I've tried to give you the true story, mostly the good and not all the bad.

I was once a caterpillar struggling to find her way, yet through the power of God and love, I have truly found my wings and am soaring through life with joy. I am convinced you can do the same!

Life gives us many rich experiences from which to draw blessings, healing, and joy. It is our job to embrace the present and release the past in order to rewrite our story. I hope your life is overflowing with love and peace that is beyond all understanding.

Lastly, I would like to conclude this book with a dare.

*Are you a daring woman?*

*If not, do you want to be one?*

*It is a very exciting journey. Will you join me?*

Daring women expectantly search for excitement and unexpected experiences. They live their lives with extreme gratitude, with purpose, and most certainly by their own rules and God's rules.

A daring woman is no longer swayed away from adventure by the needs and wants imposed on her by others, but rather focuses on the spirit within. She truly believes in herself. She lovingly acknowledges her gifts and talents to help pave the way to reach her full potential for the benefit of others.

A daring woman seeks to enrich the lives of others through the pursuit of meaningful relationships, creativity, and conscious knowledge.

A daring woman is warm, cleverly engaging, and convinced of her uniqueness so as not to ever feel threatened by the success and achievement of others.

Daring women promote themselves through authentic confidence and core style.

A daring woman does not retreat when a challenge or setback arises; rather, she embraces life's passage with courage and grace.

A daring woman knows that, truly, all things are possible with God.

A daring woman yearns to develop her inner butterfly, to find and use her butterfly wings to lead an inspired life.

So, I dare you to.

I dare you to be YOU!

## Karen Sorbo

*Entrepreneur, Fundraising Auctioneer, Motivational Speaker, Spokesperson, and Humanitarian*

Karen Sorbo transforms the serious business of raising funds for non-profit organizations into a carefully choreographed and highly entertaining event. Karen's energetic stage presence, coupled with an astute business sense, makes her one of the leading fundraising auctioneers across the United States and Mexico. Since 1993, she's conducted over 2,400 auctions, raising over 500 million for deserving organizations. Such strong outcomes are linked to Karen's knack for building empathy for the client's cause and igniting audience excitement into lively, competitive bidding.

A passionate and outspoken advocate for those in need, Karen also serves as a motivational speaker. She uses her personal triumph over childhood hardships and other traumas as encouragement. She shares with audience members how to embrace their painful past, release it, and reinvent their lives. Karen has a gift of encouraging others to forgive, seek their passion, use their gifts, and serve their purpose.

Karen has received numerous honors and recognition over the tenure of her career. In 1991, she was crowned Mrs. Minnesota International. She has been featured in several publications and on T.V. for her auction specialty. In 2003, she received the Counselor of the Year Award and was recognized by the National Auctioneers Association as one of the nation's leading fundraising auctioneers. She was selected by the Minnesota Monthly as one of the 2011 'Women of Influence." In 2012, the WSA (Women's Speaker's Association) recognized her as a "Woman you need to know."

She has two grown children and currently resides in Minnesota with her husband, Angolan native, Francelino Henriques Zau. Together they devote all their free time on international humanitarian trips making a difference, one life at a time. If you would like to support Karen's efforts to help those in need, please visit **www.karensorbofoundation.com.**

www.ingramcontent.com/pod-product-compliance
Lightning Source LLC
Chambersburg PA
CBHW060808050426
42449CB00008B/1591